# OUTWARD BOUND

# ORIENTEERING
# HANDBOOK

**Also available**
Outward Bound Backpacker's Handbook
Outward Bound Canoeing Handbook
Outward Bound First Aid Handbook
Outward Bound Map and Compass Handbook
Outward Bound Walker's Handbook
Outward Bound Rock Climbing Handbook
Outward Bound Sailing Handbook

# OUTWARD BOUND
# ORIENTEERING
# HANDBOOK

Martin Bagness

WARD LOCK

# Distance conversion table

In common with athletics events, orienteering courses are always measured in kilometres. A conversion table is given below, for those readers who are more familiar with Imperial measurements.

1km = 0.62 miles approx. 1 mile = 1.6 km approx.

| km | miles (approx.) |
|----|-----------------|
| 0.5 | 0.3 |
| 1 | 0.6 |
| 2 | 1.2 |
| 3 | 1.9 |
| 4 | 2.5 |
| 5 | 3.2 |
| 10 | 6.3 |
| 15 | 9.5 |

**A WARD LOCK BOOK**
First published in the UK in 1995
by Ward Lock
Wellington House
125 Strand
London WC2R 0BB

A Cassell Imprint

Outward Bound is a registered trade mark of the Outward Bound Trust Limited as is its device. Registration number 2876300. Registered Office: Plumtree Court, London, EC4A 4HT, England.

Distributed in Australia by
Capricorn Link (Australia) Pty Ltd
213 Carrington Road, Castle Hill,
NSW 2154

**British Library Cataloguing-in-Publication data**
A catalogue record for this book is available from the British Library

ISBN 0-7063-7362-6

Line illustrations: Martin Bagness and Sally Alexander

Map sections included courtesy of South Ribble Orienteering Club, and The Orienteering Federation of Australia.

Front cover photograph: Stephen Whitehorne

Back cover photograph: Mark Allen Publishing

Typesetting and design: Ben Cracknell

Printed and bound in Finland by Werner Söderström Oy

# Contents

# About Outward Bound®

*The Outward Bound Trust provides high-quality courses in a range of exciting outdoor activities. Our fully qualified instructors maintain the highest standards of tuition, and our safety record is second to none. Everyone who takes an Outward Bound course enjoys a rewarding and memorable experience, the benefits of which will last a lifetime.*

Outward Bound courses have been available in Britain since 1941. The original courses were the outcome of a meeting between Kurt Hahn, the educator, and Lawrence Holt, the owner of a shipping line. The marriage of the worlds of education and business is a vital feature of the Outward Bound movement. The courses are both a valuable adjunct to formal education and an important part of career development.

From its beginnings in Britain the Outward Bound movement has spread throughout the world, with 38 centres in 23 countries.

A typical course in the UK lasts from one to three weeks and may be based at one of our five national centres or take the form of an expeditionary journey by foot or by sailing boat in a wilderness setting. We run courses for all age groups, from 14 to 70!

The Outward Bound Trust also designs programmes to help companies through periods of change. This may involve developing leadership skills for young managers or assisting in building cohesive teams. The courses balance challenging outdoor tasks with reflection and review. They are specially designed so participants can translate what they gain from a course back to their working environment.

After an Outward Bound experience, people discover many positive attributes about themselves. They become more confident; they learn to share, to lead and to follow, to understand their own strengths and to work together as a group. By safeguarding each other, they form bonds of trust. They discover that many problems can be solved only with the co-operation of all members of a group.

To find out more about Outward Bound courses or to request a brochure, please contact us at the address below:

Outward Bound Trust
PO Box 1219
Windsor
Berkshire SL4 1EU

*Michael Hobbs*
Outward Bound Trust
Tel (01753) 731005

# Introduction

## What is orienteering?

Put simply, orienteering is a race where a map is used to navigate between a series of checkpoints or 'controls'. The first events were held in Sweden over 70 years ago, and since then the sport has spread around the globe – today there are over 40 member nations in the International Orienteering Federation (IOF). The rules of orienteering have evolved over the years to ensure that competition is as fair and enjoyable as possible, and the general format of events has become standardized throughout the orienteering nations, with specially drawn maps being used, which show the ground in the way which is most useful to competitors.

The map-reading side of orienteering incorporates a certain degree of cunning and improvization – it does not matter how you navigate around a course, as long as it is effective! Sometimes it pays to play safe, but at others it may be better, or more fun, to take take calculated risks. On the running side, racing through wooded terrain develops an all-round fitness involving strength, stamina, coordination and agility as well as running speed. Perhaps the fascination of orienteering stems from the fact that no one, not even a world champion, is a master of every single aspect of the sport.

At any orienteering event there is a range of courses on offer to suit different ages and levels of fitness and competitiveness. There are also courses for beginners, so that everyone can enter at the level of their choice. For this reason it is common to see children, pensioners and national team members running at the same event, although perhaps at differing speeds! So that very young children are not left out, the organizers often set out a 'string course', where the route is marked with a continuous line of streamers. In fact, orienteering has been dubbed 'The Family Sport' because it appeals to people of all generations. This is not entirely accurate, because many people attend events on their own, with friends, or as part of a school or student group. 'A Sport For All' would be a more fitting description.

Every orienteer in the world has a different set of reasons for enjoying the sport. It may be the map-reading side, or the physical challenge of running over difficult ground, or, for the very fit, the exhilaration of sprinting at full speed through forest or woodland. Some just welcome the chance to be totally independent and free to make their own decisions; for them orienteering is an escape from the 'real' world with its rules and restrictions. Or perhaps they enjoy the social scene – always lively at orienteering events the world over!

One aspect of the sport that is important to all orienteers is the scenery of forest, heath and moorland that they run through at every competition: few other sports take place in such superb natural arenas. Competitors at a recent World Student Games in Switzerland caught glimpses of snowy peaks and glaciers as they ran over alpine grassland high above the tree line; clouds of colourful parrots accompany runners in the Australian bush; navigating across Loughrigg Fell, in the English Lake District, views across lakes, woodland, meadows and mountains constantly open up in every direction.

It is hoped that this book will help to enhance all the many pleasures of orienteering, by providing beginners with the basic information that they need to make a start, and explaining advanced techniques and strategies for the experienced competitor. After all, one of the pleasures of orienteering, or any other sport for that matter, is the satisfaction that comes from learning new skills and the thrill of overcoming new challenges.

## What happens at an orienteering event?

There may be a number of different courses set out at an event, perhaps varying from 2 to 15km in length, with between 8 and 25 controls, so that each runner can choose a course appropriate to their age, experience and fitness. Runners are usually started at intervals of one or more minutes. This keeps people apart and prevents one runner from simply following another to get round the course.

At the start, each runner copies their chosen course on to their map from a master map or, at larger events, receives a map on which the course has already been printed, or 'pre-marked'. At the most usual form of event, known as a 'cross-country type', there are a number of controls set out in the terrain which must be visited in a certain order. Each control is sited at a feature on the ground which is also shown on the map, known as a 'control site'. Here there is an orange-and-white marker, in the form of a three-sided nylon box, known as a control marker, or 'kite'. Each competitor carries a control card, which is marked at each control as proof that they have completed the course.

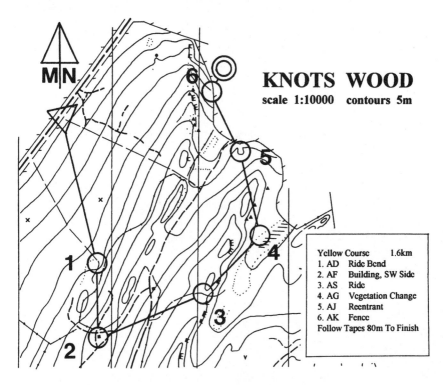

**1.1** Map of the course, description sheet and control card.

| SAFETY CHECK: This card MUST be handed in at the Finish **EVEN IF YOU RETIRE.** |||||||||
|---|---|---|---|---|---|---|---|---|

NAME *Jane Edding*
CLASS *W11* COURSE *Yellow*
CLUB *B.O.C.* START TIME *11·17*

FOR OFFICIAL USE ONLY
FINISH _____
START *11·17*
TIME _____

| 19 | 20 | 21 | 22 | 23 | 24 | 25 | 26 | 27 |
|---|---|---|---|---|---|---|---|---|
| 61 | 0Z | 1Z | ZZ | ΕZ | ΦZ | 5Z | 9Z | ΖZ |
| 10 | 11 | 12 | 13 | 14 | 15 | 16 | 17 | 18 |
| 01 | 11 | Zl | Εl | Φl | 5l | 9l | Ζl | 8l |
| 1 AD ride bend | 2 AF building | 3 AS ride | 4 AG veg. change | 5 AJ reentrant | 6 AK fence | 7 Tapes | 8 80m to finish | 9 |
| | Z | Ε | Φ | 5 | 9 | Ζ | 8 | 6 |

A control card. The orienteer has copied the information from the description sheet in the boxes on the card, in order to carry fewer pieces of paper.

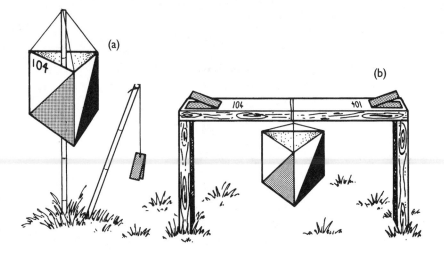

**1.2** Two different types of control marker and punch, using (a) canes and (b) a trestle. 104 is the code letter of the control site.

Competitors mark their own control card using a punch – a special clipper which is hung next to the control marker and leaves a characteristic impression of pinpricks in the card. Each runner also carries a description sheet, which gives a written description of each control feature, in case it is not clear from the map what the feature is. The description sheet also gives a control code in the form of a letter or number for each control. This code is also clearly written on the control marker to enable each runner to check that they are at the correct control site before punching their card: there may be a number of control markers set out which are on other courses. From the last control on their course runners either navigate or follow streamers to reach the finish. They are timed as they cross the finish line, and their control card is collected.

It is very important that everyone who has started a course should hand in their control card at the finish, even if they have not fully completed their course, because the collected control cards are used as a check to ensure that no one is still out in the forest at the end of the day. If the organizers believe that someone is still out, and possibly lost or injured, they will have to send out a search party.

# 1

# How to get started

## Finding out about local events

Wherever you live, there is likely to be an orienteering club organizing regular events somewhere nearby. Very often these events are announced in the local newspaper, but a better way of finding out about fixtures is to contact your nearest club. The addresses of the different National Federations, who will be able to supply the addresses of club secretaries, are given on page 104 of this book.

A typical club fixture list will provide information on the dates and starting times of all events in the region over the next few months. Orienteering events traditionally take place on a Sunday morning; however, most clubs organize a few additional events on Saturdays, and there are usually midweek events on summer evenings. The fixture list will provide a description of how to get to each event, together with a grid reference of the car park. There will also be a phone number for the organizer, in case you need some information that is not given in the details.

## Choosing a first event

When taking your first steps in orienteering, it is generally better to choose a small, low-key event. Look for events which are advertised as 'Local' or 'Evening' events. 'Colour-coded' events, which feature a range of courses of different lengths and difficulties graded with a colour system, also provide an ideal introduction to the sport.

The orienteering calendar will also feature a number of larger events, such as 'Badge' or 'National' events. It is often necessary to enter these in advance, by sending in a special entry form. These events attract many more competitors – up to 2000 in some cases – and as the atmosphere is less informal it may be harder to seek help and advice than at smaller events. Despite this, it is still quite possible to make a start at a larger event: many will feature a range of short colour-coded courses which can be entered on the day rather than in advance.

## Permanent courses

Shortly before the start of an orienteering event, the courses are set out by placing markers at control sites. The markers are then removed as soon as the event is over, and the area may not be used again for several months or even years. In contrast, at a permanent course there are always markers in place, usually in the form of sturdy wooden posts. Orienteers can turn up at any time and obtain a 'map pack', which contains a map showing the locations of the markers and a number of suggested courses of varying difficulty, plus other information about the location.

Permanent courses are an ideal way of gaining an introduction to the sport. There is no need to wait for a local event to be staged; a permanent course can be visited at any time that suits you. Many people are also put off by the element of competition and pressure at an organized event, where everyone is timed around a course, and they may prefer to start out at their own pace, when there is no one around to see them take their first steps with a map and compass. Permanent courses are not timed and are non-competitive, although it is sometimes possible to obtain a certificate on completing a course.

Permanent courses are set up in a variety of different locations, ranging from forests to local parks, and may be managed by bodies such as forestry authorities, local councils or even orienteering clubs themselves. Map packs can usually be purchased at a shop or café near the start of the course. There are permanent courses in many scenic regions, and these are often visited by holidaymakers, especially families. Some attract large numbers of visitors seeking to add variety to a sightseeing or walking holiday.

Information on permanent courses can be obtained from the National Federations (see Useful addresses) and from local clubs.

## Courses in orienteering at outdoor centres

Some outdoor centres run courses exclusively in orienteering, or teach orienteering as part of a general outdoor activities course. Although the majority of orienteers are introduced to the sport through local events or permanent courses, tuitional courses offer an excellent alternative. It is possible to obtain a thorough grounding in the basics of orienteering over a week-long or even a weekend course. Addresses of centres running accredited courses in orienteering can be obtained from the National Federations (see Useful addresses). Courses including orienteering are run at Outward Bound centres around the world.

# 2

# Taking part in an orienteering event

Taking part is the best way to pick up the basic skills of orienteering and to understand how the sport is organized. The more advanced techniques and methods of training, discussed later in this book, are best practised when you have already run a few courses and are familiar with the way in which events are staged. This chapter explains the procedure at a typical event. Around the world, orienteering events are organized on very similar lines. The procedure at an event may seem complicated at first, especially when described on paper, but at an actual event things quickly start to make sense, and there are usually people around who are happy to help.

## Getting there
The event details given in a newspaper or published in the fixtures list sent out by a local club will usually provide travel directions. Events are often signed from the nearest main road, village or other landmark; road signs usually take the form of arrows or red and white markers. Unfortunately it is often difficult to reach orienteering events by public transport. This is partly due to the remote location of many venues, and partly due to the infrequency of buses and trains on Sundays, which is when the majority of events take place. There is often no alternative but to travel by car; however, if you belong to an orienteering club it is usually possible to arrange a lift with other competitors, and school and college groups frequently organize coaches or minibuses to events.

## Registration
### Choosing a course
The first thing to do on arrival at an event is to register for a course. Look for 'Event Registration' which is usually situated in a tent or parked car. Before registering, you will need to choose which course to enter. A sign listing the courses available, together with their lengths in kilometres, will usually be on display. But beware – orienteering courses take considerably longer to complete than you would at first

expect, judging by their length. A course of 5km say, will take a lot longer to complete than a straightforward run of the same distance because you will have to negotiate terrain which may be overgrown, muddy, hilly, or all three! In addition, navigation is always time-consuming, even if all goes well.

Most local events use a colour-coding system. Details of the British colour-coding system are given on page 106. Other countries use similar systems but the British system has been used in this book as an example of how coding systems work. White and yellow standard courses are most suitable for young children who are beginners. An orange standard course would be suitable for an adult beginner, although if you are reasonably fit and are used to other forms of map-reading (for example, if you have used maps while walking) a red course would be suitably challenging. The other courses usually available – green, blue and brown – are longer or more technically difficult, and are suitable for experienced orienteers.

Many beginners prefer to enter their first few events as a group of two or three. Although most experienced orienteers prefer to run on their own, there is usually no problem in entering a short colour-coded course as a pair or in a group of three or four people. It can be rewarding and good fun to share the learning process with some friends – provided, of course, that there are no major disagreements out on the course about where to go next!

At registration you will be asked to pay an entry fee, and in return you will receive a control card with your start time written on it, a control description sheet for your course, and a blank map of the competition area.

### Choosing a start time

At registration you will be asked when you would like to start. When working out your start time, you should find out how long it takes to get to the start, which may be between 2 and 20 minutes' walking time away, and then add to this at least a further 30 minutes for getting ready.

## Getting ready to start

Unfortunately, orienteering involves carrying several pieces of paper with you; the map, control card and description sheet. Many orienteers simplify things by copying the information from the description sheet on to the control card before they start, so that the code and

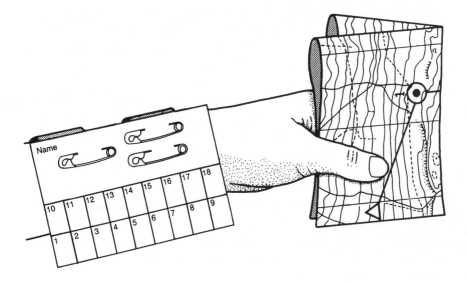

**2.1** How to hold the map, with the control card attached to the wrist.

description for control number one are copied into box number one on the control card, and so on (see figure 1.1).

Before setting off for the start it is wise to put the map into a suitably sized map case, which is a clear plastic bag that will protect the map from water, mud and the ravages of whatever kinds of vegetation you could end up battling through on the course. The map case should not be rigid, as it is important to be able to fold the map down to a handy size when orienteering. You should hold the map in your hand the whole time while out on the course, so that you can refer to it constantly. The control card should be firmly attached to you in some way, either pinned to your sleeve or front, or to a wrist band, or fixed to a wrist loop. It must be easily accessible; removing it from a pocket, for example, is fiddly and wastes time at each control. Some control cards are printed on plastic paper, but if the card is made from ordinary cardboard it should be protected with a small plastic bag (you can punch through the plastic at each control) or covered with a clear adhesive plastic. At some events you may be required to carry a whistle to summon assistance if you are injured and cannot move. Use a safety pin to fix the whistle out of the way in a pocket or inside your clothing.

Having changed and sorted out your map, map case, control card and descriptions, you are just about ready to set off for the start, but first it is worth making a quick check to see that you have everything. Run through a mental check-list including compass, map, control card, descriptions, red pen, whistle, and anything else you may need, such as spectacles or contact lenses.

Many orienteers jog to the start as a way of warming up. Once at the start, you will probably have a few minutes to wait before your start time is announced and this provides an opportunity to do some stretching exercises (see Chapter 10).

## At the start

Next to the start there will probably be a display clock showing race time, and there may be an official shouting the time at each minute. When your start time is called you should enter the first 'start box', which will be marked out with tapes. At some events a small detachable stub section may be removed from your control card as a record that you have started. Most events use a 'minus three minute' system, which means that there are three start boxes and you move forward into the next box at each minute until you reach the actual start line. Do not worry if this sounds complicated; there will always be someone around to help. There may be several people starting at the same time as you: each person on a different course.

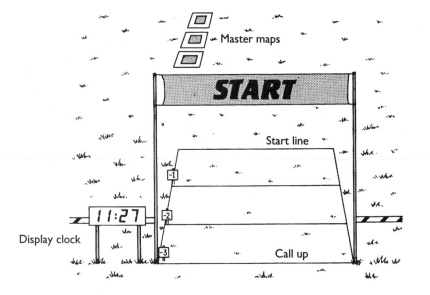

**2.2** Start layout showing the start boxes for a 'minus three minute' system.

## At the master maps

From the start line there will be a taped route leading to the master maps, where you copy the course on to your own map (occasionally you may be able to copy down your course before starting, in your own time). It is best to copy down the course exactly as it is shown on the master map, using a triangle to show the start, drawing a circle around each control feature, and using a double circle to show the finish. Do not make the control circles too small, as they will tend to obscure detail around the control feature. Number each control and link each circle with a straight line, so that there is no confusion about the order in which to visit them, and no chance of accidentally forgetting to visit a control.

Take care not to rush at the master maps, even though you are copying down the course in race time. It is well worth double-checking what you have copied, as it is disastrous to copy the position of a control incorrectly. If you are introducing a young child to orienteering, you will probably be allowed to visit the master maps with them, to help them copy down the course.

Once you have copied down the course, away you go.

## At the finish

After the description for the last control on your control description sheet, it will say either 'Navigate to the finish' or 'Follow tapes to the finish'. Either way, you will soon find yourself crossing the finish line, where an official will collect your control card. There will usually be a cup of orange juice waiting, and there will certainly be a group of other orienteers, still buzzing with excitement after their runs, eager to discuss their triumphs, silly mistakes, and the relative merits of different routes. A short while later, perhaps after you have got changed, your result will have been calculated and the punch marks on your control card checked. The results are usually displayed as paper slips stapled to a string or as a computer printout, and full lists are generally posted out during the week following the event. To receive a copy, you may have to fill out an envelope before leaving the event.

# 3

# Equipment

## Clothing

If you are about to take your first steps in orienteering, choose clothes that are light, do not absorb lots of water, and allow plenty of freedom of movement. At most events you will be required to wear long trousers, to cut down on the risk of infections being spread through cuts and scratches. Tracksuit trousers are fine, together with a T-shirt, tracksuit top or waterproof, depending on the weather.

Experienced orienteers prefer to wear 'orienteering suits' ('O-suits') made from thin nylon. These are ideal in every way, except that they tend to look like pyjamas! Lycra tights are also popular, and are certainly more stylish. Some orienteers wear gaiters or strengthened socks known as 'bramble bashers', to protect their legs from the undergrowth. All specialized items of orienteering clothing and equipment can be bought from mobile shops at the larger events.

## Footwear

The ideal footwear has a good grip and is light, non-absorbent and well fitting. Trainers or lightweight boots are fine at first, but after a few events you may feel the need to get some special orienteering shoes, which are usually light and strongly made. The soles will feature deep studs, although some faster runners prefer spiked shoes (similar to track or cross-country spikes but more robust). A hybrid sole, where each stud is tipped with a tiny, hardwearing spike, has recently become popular.

The most important consideration when choosing a shoe is the tightness of fit. Obviously, if a shoe is too tight it will be very uncomfortable and may cause blisters, but loose-fitting shoes are equally unsuitable as they provide little support on uneven ground, which increases the risk of a sprained ankle, that most common and frustrating of orienteering injuries.

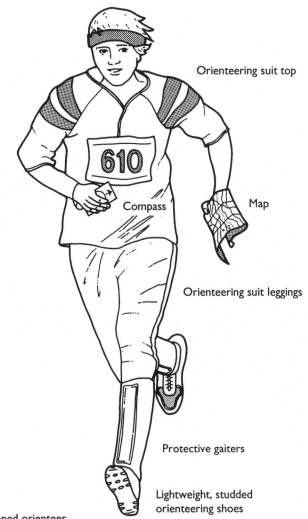

Orienteering suit top

Compass

Map

Orienteering suit leggings

Protective gaiters

Lightweight, studded orienteering shoes

**3.1** The fully equipped orienteer.

## Other equipment

Apart from clothing and footwear, there are a number of other items that are essential or useful. Most orienteers keep these items together in a bag or box.

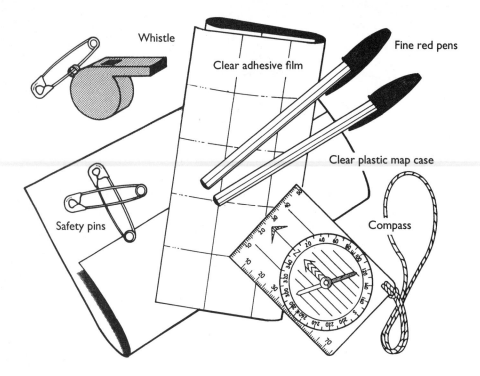

**3.2** Equipment for orienteering.

---

## Equipment checklist

- **Compass** – see Chapter 5
- **Map cases** – clear plastic bags of various sizes, for protecting the map
- **Red pens** – either ballpoints or very fine permanent ink pens, for copying the course on to the map
- **Adhesive plastic film** or plastic control-card case – for protecting the control card
- **Safety pins** – for attaching the control card
- **Whistle** – compulsory at some events as a means of summoning help in an emergency
- **Watch**
- **First aid kit** – see page 85

# 4

# Map-reading skills

## Orienteering maps

Orienteering events almost always use specially drawn maps. The first events in Great Britain, for instance, which took place in the late 1960s, were staged using the official government-survey maps, but orienteers soon began to modify these by drawing in extra footpaths and then taking photocopies. Eventually, maps were completely redrawn and then printed in five colours to include many additional features of use to the runner. During the last 25 years, orienteering maps have become more and more refined, with the ultimate aim of making competition as fair and enjoyable as possible. Orienteers from many nations have contributed to this process, and map scales and symbols have now been standardized across the world.

### *Scales*

The map scales most commonly used are 1:15 000 and 1:10 000. At these scales the map is clear to read and can be printed on a manageably small piece of paper. 1:15 000 is usually used for major events, while 1:10 000 maps are clearer to read and are used for teaching orienteering, or where the terrain is especially complex, or for the older age classes where failing eyesight can be a problem. Scales of 1:2500 or 1:5000 are occasionally used for maps of very small areas, such as parks or school grounds.

When using these scales, many people are surprised at how quickly they cover distances. This is especially true for people who have used walking or road maps in the past and are used to scales of 1:25 000 and 1:50 000. Due to the scales used, an orienteering map printed on a large piece of paper will depict a relatively small area: the average orienteering area is perhaps 2 × 3km in extent. Fit beginners have been known to overshoot their first control and then keep going until they reach the edge of the forest, before realizing that something has gone wrong!

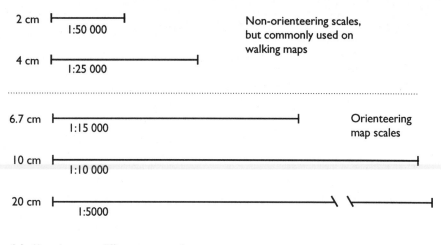

**4.1** 1km shown at different map scales.

---

## Map scales

- **1:15 000** 1cm on the map represents 150m on the ground.
  The north lines on the map are printed 500m apart.

- **1:10 000** 1cm on the map represents 100m on the ground.
  The north lines on the map are printed 250m apart.

- **1:5000** 1cm on the map represents 50m on the ground.

- **1:2500** 1cm on the map represents 25m on the ground.

---

## Symbols

On an orienteering map, white is used to show wooded land. Varying shades of green are used to show dense woodland that is difficult to get through; the darker the green, the thicker the forest. Bright yellow shows cultivated fields or open grassland, and pale yellow shows rough open land, such as moorland. This is in contrast to most other forms of mapping, where white shows open land and green shows forest.

A key to the International Map Symbols is provided in figure 4.2. As a rough guide, black symbols show features which are generally man-made, such as roads, footpaths, fences, walls, power lines, railways, buildings and settlements. Black symbols are also used to depict rock features such as boulders, rocky ground, crags and cliffs. Blue symbols show water features such as lakes, rivers, streams and marshes. Brown

## BLACK SYMBOLS

motorway
main road
minor road
car park
dirt road
vehicle track
large footpath
small footpath
wide ride
narrow ride
railway
major powerline
powerline
stone wall
ruined wall
high fence
fence
riuned fence
gate or stile
buildings
ruins
firing range
large tower
small tower
fodder rack
cairn
trig point
high cliffs
small cliffs
rocky pit
cave
boulders
large boulders
boulder field
stony ground

## YELLOW SYMBOLS

open land
semi open land
rough open land

## BROWN SYMBOLS

contour
index contour
downslope tag
form line
steep bank
boundary bank
erosion gully
small gully
knolls
small knolls
depressions
small depressions
pits
broken ground
platforms

## BLUE SYMBOLS

lake
ponds
water hole
uncrossable river
wide stream
small stream
ditch
uncrossable marsh
marsh
seasonal marsh
narrow marsh
water tank

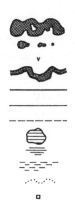

## GREEN SYMBOLS

undergrowth: slow
undergrowth: walk
run
forest: slow run
forest: walk
forest: impenetrable
run in one direction

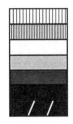

**4.2** Key to International Map Symbols.

contour lines show ground features which are largely natural, such as knolls, depressions, ridges and valleys.

Some map symbols have been introduced to make competition fairer; for example, when choosing a good route it is very important to know where dense forest, depicted as green, will be found. Similarly, marshes and rocky ground are likely to be slower going. Other features are shown on the map to provide detail by which to navigate, or to provide control sites; these features might be quite small, such as boulders or pits. As a general rule, if a feature is big enough to be seen by someone running close by, then it is shown on the map, but if it is so small that the runner has to stop and search for it, then it is not shown.

Although map symbols are standardized across the world, many regions use one or two special symbols of their own to show features that are unique to that area. For example, in the oak woodlands native to the English Lake District, there are numerous circular platforms which were once the sites of charcoal burners' camps, part of a local industry that died out about 50 years ago. These features are easily visible and are useful to the orienteer, so are depicted with a brown triangle.

## Making orienteering maps

Orienteering maps are made either by keen amateurs, who are usually members of an orienteering club, or by professional surveyors specializing in the production of orienteering maps. The mapper starts out with an existing map or with a special 'plot' made from air photos, and then walks around the area adding and updating relevant detail. He or she has two main concerns: firstly to map features accurately in exactly the right positions, secondly to show the ground in a way that makes sense and looks right to the runner. Contour features are often exaggerated to depict the apparent shape of the ground, while other features may be omitted if they are felt to be insignificant – showing too much detail would clutter the map and make it less easy to read. Although the map has to be very accurate, there is still room for a certain degree of artistic licence, and many mappers have their own distinctive 'style'. Once an area has been surveyed, the map is drawn up using pen and ink, by scribing (scraping lines on a plastic-coated film), or using a computer, ready for printing.

Many orienteers have found that map-making has helped them to improve their own orienteering, as they become aware of the problems a mapper faces in depicting the ground. When orienteering, it is often useful to be able to 'see into the mapper's head'.

# Map-reading basics

Orienteering navigation is a combination of map-reading and compass skills. Compass skills are explained in the next chapter; the rudiments of map-reading are dealt with here.

## *Setting and thumbing the map*

Setting the map, sometimes known as 'orientating the map', means holding it so that the features on the map are lined up with the same features on the ground. Rather than always keeping the north edge of the map at the top and the writing the right way up, as you would do when reading a newspaper, turn the map so that it always matches the ground. As you change direction, you will have to turn the map in your hand – a bit like using the steering wheel of a car. Keep the map set all the time when you are orienteering.

With the map set, it is much easier to visualize the relative positions of the features ahead of you: which side of you they will be on, whether you need to turn right or left at the next path junction, and so

**4.3** Setting and thumbing the map, so that the features on the map are lined up with the same features on the ground and the thumb is always right next to where you are.

on. The map can also be set with the compass, and this is explained in the next chapter.

Thumbing the map means holding it so that your thumb is always right next to where you are. To do this, you will have to keep changing the position of your thumb on the map as you move over the ground. You will also need to keep the map folded to a fairly small size. Thumbing the map means that you can always see your position at a glance, and helps your eyes to focus quickly on the right place.

Most orienteers hold the map in their left hand and the compass in their right. There is no reason why this is any better than doing it the other way round – it is simply a matter of personal preference – so choose the method that feels most comfortable.

## Using line features

Line features, sometimes called 'handrails', are things such as roads, paths, fences and streams that are easy to follow. All orienteers use line features to simplify navigation, but they are of most use to the beginner. The easier colour-coded courses – white and yellow – are set with all the controls on line features, thereby making it possible to follow line features the whole way round the course.

During your first event it is a good idea to keep things simple by sticking to line features as much as possible. Make sure that you do not run past path junctions without seeing them – it is easily done! Keep thinking ahead so that you know which way to turn at the next junction and keep the map set with the feature you are following. Never rush, and take time to get used to the way features represented on the map appear on the ground. Think about the scale of the map; it may help to say to yourself how far you expect to run before you reach the next path junction; for example, 'It looks about 1cm on the map, so it should be about 100m on the ground – that's about two lengths of a swimming pool.'

## Into the terrain: leaving line features

At a colour-coded event, the orange and red courses will be planned so that most of the controls are not sited on line features but are placed some way into the terrain, on features such as ruined buildings, pits or boulders. If you have just started orienteering, always try to follow the easiest routes, do not leave the line features until you are as close as possible to the control. It is a good idea to find an easily recognizable feature, or 'attack point', from which to strike into the wilder areas. On some legs you may have no alternative but to choose a route which is

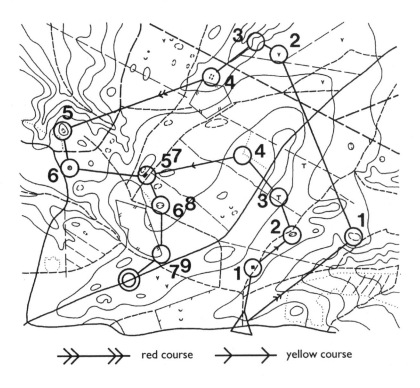

→→→ red course    →→ yellow course

**4.4** Examples of yellow- and red-standard courses: note the relative number of line features incorporated in each.

mostly through these, but you may still be able to simplify things by picking up sections of line features on the way. Some contour features, such as ridges and valleys, may provide useful handrails to follow, and you may also see small features such as thickets, clearings and marshes to confirm that you are running in the right direction. When running straight through the terrain it is important to use your compass as a back-up to map-reading (see Chapter 5).

## Forming a mental picture

The best orienteers can take in more information from a single glance at the map than less experienced orienteers because they can form an instant mental picture of the ground ahead, but this takes a lot of practice. Map-reading is like learning a foreign language: at first, you have to translate phrases back into English in order to understand them, but as you become fluent you know what they mean straightaway.

When looking at the map, try to picture the features on either side of your route, as well as those in front of you. It helps to take frequent glances at the map, rather than trying to remember a large chunk in one go. Try to visualize where features lie relative to one another; for example, rather than saying to yourself, 'I will pass a marsh, a clearing and a hut', imagine these features as a picture – the marsh may form a crescent shape around the front of the clearing, with the hut situated on the back edge of the clearing. The most useful feature when forming a mental picture is the shape of the ground shown by contour lines. Using contours for navigation is explained in Chapter 7, and more advanced map-reading skills in Chapter 9.

In the early days, orienteering maps showed relatively little detail and it was easiest to navigate by accurate compass bearings and careful distance estimation. Although these methods are still very useful in some circumstances, detailed modern maps now enable the orienteer to use map-reading to a much greater degree. Following the features on the map is usually a faster and more reliable way of navigating; it is also very satisfying when you find yourself running through an area which is just how you pictured it to be from the map. Orienteers sometimes describe this feeling after a successful run, explaining how 'the map and the ground became one'.

## *1994 British Relay Championships,*
### HEYSHOTT COMMON, SUSSEX, ENGLAND

Julia wondered what was she doing here, standing in a field somewhere in Sussex, hundreds of miles from home. She normally only went orienteering two or three times a year, usually to local events organized by her club, Warrior OC. She enjoyed the sport – it made a change from fell running or rock climbing – but did not consider herself to be an expert. Yet here she was, surrounded by hundreds of enthusiasts who seemed to know exactly what they were doing. To make matters worse, she was due to run second leg in the competitive Women's Open category, and the other two girls in her team, Heather and Yvette, were members of the British squad. In fact, they had finished first and second in the Individual Championships the day before.

Relay competitions are usually open to teams of three, or sometimes four, runners. They follow the same format as track relays in athletics; the first loop runner completes their course, then hands over to the second loop runner, who completes their course, and so on. All the first loop runners set off together in a 'mass start', so the team that finishes first is the winner. Relays are always fast, furious and good fun to take part in.

Heather was to run the first loop for the Warrior team. She ran first loop for the British team in international races, and was keen to test her relay running with a forthcoming World Cup race in mind. Yvette, Britain's best female orienteer and ranked second in the world, would run the final anchor loop.

The other girls had told Julia not to worry if she did not do well – they would still enjoy their runs – but she felt that she could not let them down, especially as Yvette had taken the trouble to walk around the assembly field with her to point out the last control, the change-over and the run-out, and had given her plenty of advice on relay running and on how to orienteer in this type of heathland terrain.

While Heather was out running the first loop, Julia decided to work out a plan of action based on the advice Yvette had given her, and on what she felt to be her strengths and weaknesses. She knew from her results as a fell runner that she could run strongly. Yvette had told her that the area would be criss-crossed with sandy paths, so she decided to keep to paths as much as possible and make the most of her running ability. She would not try anything too fancy, like taking short cuts between footpaths, unless there was no alternative. This fitted in with Yvette's advice that the second loop runner should be safe rather than fast. She resolved to follow the map carefully, even when she was on a path, and to tick off features as she passed them.

Heather had told her to watch what other orienteers were doing – they often gave away the positions of controls – but always to check that the control code on the marker matched the code on her description sheet before punching her control card, as there would be a lot of markers out in the heathland, many of them on other courses. It would not do to disqualify the team by visiting the wrong control!

Another club member gave Julia some advice on how to 'flow' through controls quickly and save time by planning ahead, but she decided to ignore this in order to keep things as simple and as safe as possible. Having worked out her plan she felt relaxed and positive.

Heather came back in second place and handed over to Julia, who set off into the heathland. She played it safe to the first control, carefully keeping the map set with the ground and ticking off features as she passed them. Fortunately, a path led to within 100m of the control feature, and there was a distinct bend in the path which she chose as an 'attack point'. As she left the path bend she was pleased to find that the features around the control were just as she had pictured them to be from the map. Things went less smoothly on the way

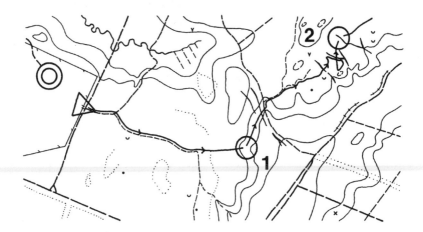

**4.5** Part of Julia's route in the 1994 British Relay Championships.

to number two, however. Feeling confident, she started to run faster and began to ignore the map detail. She lost track of the bends and junctions on the tiny footpath she was following, and started to look for the control feature, a gully, about 50m too soon. It took her several minutes to sort out where she was and to find the right feature. As she checked the code on the marker and punched her control card she felt briefly angry with herself and resolved not to make any more mistakes. From now on she would stick to her plan at all costs.

Julia completed the remaining ten legs on the course carefully and steadily and with no other mishaps. She enjoyed running across the heathland terrain, with its sandy hills, heathery clearings and scattered pine and birch trees. Although unfamiliar, it seemed easier than the rough forests and moorlands that she was used to running on, with more handrail features to simplify navigation.

Julia finished her loop in sixth place. Yvette ran the final loop, in what was the fastest time of the day by three minutes, to pull the Warrior team up to a final position of third. The winners were three Sheffield girls, running for South Yorkshire Orienteers. Yvette and Heather were delighted with Julia's run, and impressed that she could do so well with relatively little experience of orienteering. Julia was pleased and relieved that her plan of careful map-reading and safe route choice had paid off. She had not let the others down, and would return home with the surprise bonus of a bronze medal.

# 5

# Compass skills

Chapter 4 introduced the basics of using the map. This chapter deals with the other major element of orienteering navigation: the compass.

The compass becomes most important when the terrain is flat and vague and a lack of features make it difficult to follow the map, for instance when you are heading for a small control feature in an otherwise empty, featureless area. It should always be used as a back-up, however, even when you are able to navigate by following features on the map. When you are running along a path it is often worth glancing at the compass as well, to check that it is in fact the right path, and that you are going in the right direction.

It is easy to learn the simple procedures for using a compass – much easier than learning to read a map, which requires a great deal of practice. Yet most mistakes are caused by ignoring the compass. The compass is always right, whereas it is easy to be misled by the map.

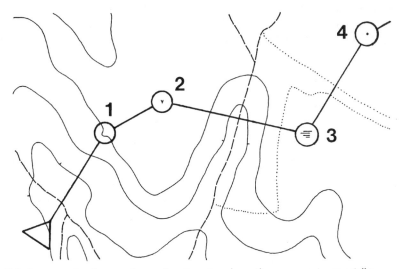

**5.1** An example of vague, featureless terrain, where the compass is especially important.

## Orienteering compasses

The majority of orienteers use a protractor-type compass. This is a hand-held compass with a rotatable housing set in a plastic baseplate. Compasses of this type are also widely used by walkers and mountaineers. There is no point in using a model with a very large baseplate; a medium-sized compass is easier to carry and use. In the last few years, compasses have been developed with needles which settle in position remarkably quickly. Although these are expensive, they are popular with top competitors, who look at the compass 'on the run', that is without stopping running.

Some orienteers use a thumb compass, which is fixed to the side of the thumb with an elastic strap. They are used slightly differently to ordinary compasses (see page 35).

## Three ways of using the compass

The following are the three most commonly used methods of working with a compass. There is no need to learn all three: simply find the method that suits you best and seems to work well. It does not matter what kind of compass you use or how you use it, as long as you use it frequently and effectively.

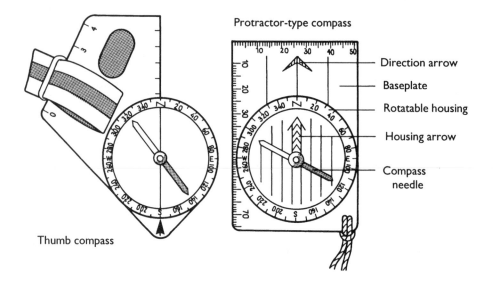

Protractor-type compass

Direction arrow

Baseplate

Rotatable housing

Housing arrow

Compass needle

Thumb compass

**5.2** Thumb and protractor-type compasses.

**5.3** Setting the map with the compass.

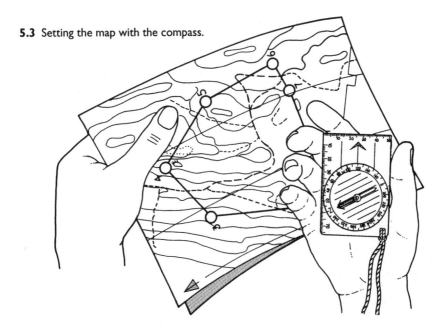

## Setting the map with the compass

Chapter 4 explained how to set the map using the features on the ground. The map can also be set with the compass, by simply turning the map until the north lines on the map are lined up with the compass needle. There is no need to move the compass housing or to look at any of the arrows drawn on to the compass. Whether the map is set using the ground or using the compass, the north edge of the map will always end up facing north, and all the features on the map and on the ground will be lined up the same way.

The compass is useful for setting the map when there are no visible ground features that can be used. It is always a good idea to set the map with the compass when you are lost, as this makes it easier to fit the map to the ground features around you when you are working out your position.

When the map is set, an imaginary line drawn on the map between you and your desired destination will point in the direction in which you need to run. In this way you can find out roughly which direction to follow by just lining up the compass needle with the north lines on the map. There is no need to do anything more complicated unless you need to be more accurate, in which case you may decide that it would be a good idea to take a bearing.

## Taking a compass bearing

At first glance the protractor compass is a confusing instrument, with several different lines and arrows marked on the housing and baseplate. However, the process of taking a bearing is a simple one and is explained in three stages in figure 5.4.

Taking a bearing is most useful when you need to be accurate, for instance when you are looking for a small control feature in an otherwise featureless area. An accurate bearing is also useful when you are crossing an area of dense forest where there is a low level of visibility.

Although some orienteers only take a bearing when they need to be very accurate, others prefer to take a bearing on every leg of the course. This is because they find it reassuring to employ a safe routine. Whether you take bearings all the time, or instead use the other, rougher, compass methods described in this chapter, combined with bearings when you need to be more accurate, is a matter of personal preference.

The accuracy of a bearing depends on the care you take when making sightings (step 3 of figure 5.4). If you want to be extremely accurate then you should stand still, try to hold the compass level, and take a sighting on a feature as far away as possible.

Many experienced orienteers save time by looking at the compass without stopping running. This technique is vital for success at a high level, yet it is often poorly executed. It helps to hold the compass in a steady, level position for a couple of seconds *before* glancing at it, to give the needle a chance to settle. A common mistake is to try to follow the compass direction arrow, rather than using it to take a sighting on something in the distance – it is essential to look beyond the compass when following a bearing.

## Running on the needle

This is it not as painful as it sounds! In fact, it is a way of saving time and using the compass roughly, as a back-up to map-reading. If you wish to run due north or due south then there is no need to set the compass, as all you need to do is follow the compass needle (remembering that the red end points north, and the white end south). You can use the same principle to run due east or west, as shown in figure 5.5.

Some orienteers extend this technique to cover bearings in any direction. They look at the map to see what angle the leg they are running makes with the north lines, then turn the whole compass until the needle makes the same angle with the direction arrow.

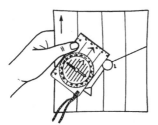

I   Place the compass on the map with the edge of the baseplate alongside the line you wish to follow.

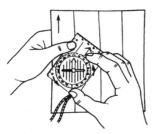

2   Rotate the housing until the housing arrow is aligned with the north lines on the map.

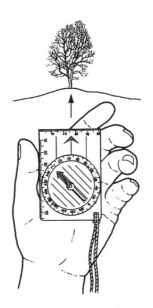

3   Taking a sighting: hold the compasss level and steady. Turn the whole compass *and* yourself until the needle is aligned with the housing arow. The compass is now pointing in your direction of travel.

**5.4** Taking a compass bearing.

## Using a thumb compass

The thumb compass is held in the same hand as the map. The edge of the compass is kept aligned with the leg you are running on the map, and the compass needle is kept aligned with the north lines on the map. This means that the map is always set with the compass and the ground, and the line of the leg on the map is always pointing in the direction you need to follow. Some thumb compasses are made with a rotatable housing, so that it is possible to use them like a protractor compass to take a bearing if you need to be especially accurate.

The advantages of the thumb compass are that the map is automatically set all the time, which makes map-reading easier, and you can always see which direction to run in. In addition, you can keep one hand free for opening gates, waving at friends, and so on. The disadvantages are that the map has to be refolded continually so that the compass can be positioned for each leg. The compass may also obscure detail on the map, and it can be hard to thumb the map accurately.

The thumb compass employs a clever and simple system, but it still has to be used with skill and care to be effective.

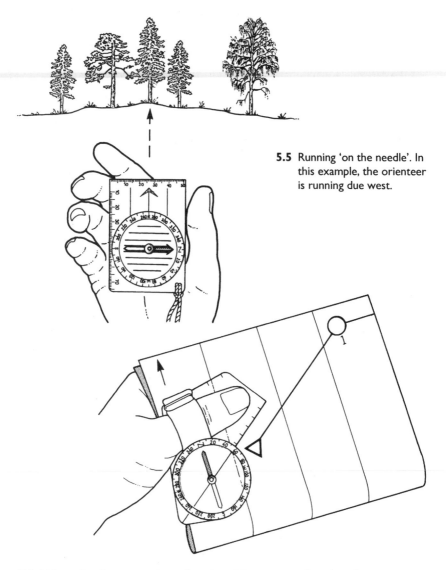

**5.5** Running 'on the needle'. In this example, the orienteer is running due west.

**5.6** Using a thumb compass: keep the edge of the compass aligned on the map with the leg you are running, and the compass needle aligned with the north lines.

## The 1985 World Orienteering Championships,
### KOOYOORA STATE PARK, AUSTRALIA

Colin jogged the final few metres to the start line, which was hidden amongst the gum trees well away from the bustle of the warm-up area. He had been called forward to the start only two minutes before his start time, to prevent him from seeing the direction earlier runners were taking to the first control. Over the last two years he had run several thousand miles in training for this race, and had mentally rehearsed this moment again and again. He knew the course would be long and technically demanding. The start clock gave a five-second countdown, then a final beep. As Colin grabbed his map and took his first steps into the forest he suddenly relaxed. His nerves vanished and were replaced with feelings of confidence and determination. At last he had started, he was orienteering, and this was *his* day!

The World Championships take place every two years. They are the most prestigious event in the orienteering calendar, with each nation being allowed to send only its best five men and five women athletes. In 1985 the World Championships were held in the southern hemisphere for the first time. The athletes had been taken to the venue of the race by bus early that morning. The location of the forest had been kept a closely guarded secret; even as the bus left the country town of Bendigo and headed northwards the runners were unaware of their destination.

The first thing Colin did was locate the start triangle on the map. A glance at the first leg told him that the best route was a straight line. There were no paths to follow, and no major obstacles to avoid such as thickets or steep hills. The map showed a bewildering mass of detail, mostly crags and boulders, but despite this he felt confident. He knew that he could rely on the strongest part of his technique: the compass. He had spent the previous year living and racing in Scandinavia, the home of the world's best orienteers, and competing in the trackless forests of Sweden had forced him to perfect his compass skills. Although he used only a small, simple thumb compass, he was confident in his ability to run straight and fast.

Colin knew that as long as he kept to his plan of accurate compass it would be relatively easy to follow the map. He was aware that other runners would wander from  the straight line, and as a result would have considerably more trouble in fitting the map to the ground; they would only be aware that they were somewhere in a broad corridor, whereas he knew that he would be close to the straight line. If he saw, say, a cluster of boulders or a knoll it would be much easier to locate it on the map.

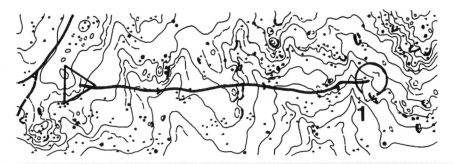

**5.7** Colin's straight-line route from the start to the first control at the 1985 World Championships.

Colin ran fast on the first two legs, managing to relate the map to the complex terrain. The third leg was short, about 200m, and half-way to the control he realized that he could no longer fit the map to the ground. He was confident in his compass, so rather than stop to work out his position he continued to run hard. Still the map did not make sense, but a second later, still unaware of his position on the map, he jumped down a small rock step almost landing on the control marker. Colin knew that there was more to it than luck though – his compass had saved him a few times in the past in a similar way when his map-reading had let him down. He was well aware that if he kept close to the straight-line route he would not go far wrong.

Colin kept to his plan of straight running for the remainder of the 15km course, with no other worrying moments. As he settled into the course he began to enjoy the orienteering. The terrain chosen by the Australian organizers was weirdly beautiful. Clumps of pink granite boulders lay strewn across the forest, some perfectly spherical like huge ball-bearings, others mushroom-shaped or squashed together to form tors rising above the trees like great piles of pancakes. The area was a natural wilderness, heavily forested with tall, white-trunked eucalyptus trees. There were few man-made features to simplify the map-reading, just the shape of the ground and the granite outcrops. White cockatoos screeched noisily from the highest branches of dead gum trees, and at one point Colin saw a group of kangaroos bound into a thicket of yellow and green wattle bushes.

Colin finished the World Championships in a fine twelfth position. At the time, this was one of the best results ever achieved by a non-Scandinavian runner. His tactics of running straight and his skill with the compass had contributed to a near-perfect run in exceptionally demanding terrain.

# 6

# Distance estimation

This chapter deals with methods of estimating how far you have run. Chapter 5 explained how the compass can give an accurate and reliable measure of direction; unfortunately, there is no handy instrument that gives a similar measure of distance, so knowing how far you have run is more a matter of estimation than of accurate measurement.

In most areas there is enough detail for you to determine how far you have run by following features on the map. However, when the terrain is vague and featureless, or when you are heading for a small control feature in an area of only a few details, it is useful to be able to estimate the distance you have covered.

## Pace counting

Pace counting is a method of estimating the distance you have run by keeping a mental count of the number of paces you have used. Pace counting is often used in conjunction with an accurate compass bearing in order to find a tricky control.

It is best to mention straightaway that pace counting is not everyone's cup of tea. Many orienteers rarely use pace counting because they find that counting in their head takes away the feeling of fun and freedom that they get when running. Pace counting also makes it more difficult to concentrate on the other aspects of navigation. You may prefer to use pace counting only as a last resort measure, a technique that you have at your disposal yet only put into practice on those few occasions when compass and map-reading do not suffice.

Pace counting is a simple technique to learn. First of all, you need to work out how many paces you use to cover 100m. You can find this out by running a measured distance in forest terrain at your normal speed. It is better to count 'double paces', in other words only when your left or right foot hits the ground. When you decide to pace count during a competition, you first of all need to measure the distance that you intend to cover from the map, and then work out how many paces you expect to use to cover that distance. For example, if you use 80

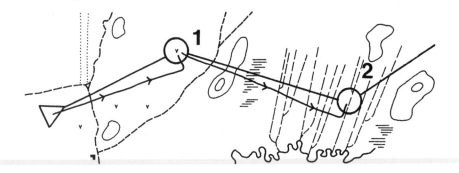

**6.1** Situations where distance estimation is important. The first control is a small
feature in otherwise featureless terrain; the second is on a ditch among many
similar ditches. The orienteer's route shows use of accurate compass, together
with distance estimation, to 'aim off' deliberately to one side of the control in
order to know which way to turn to locate the marker.

paces to cover 100m, and you wish to run for 300m, then you will
need to count 240 paces, or 120 double paces. You may have to add
extra paces if the leg is uphill or across unusually rough ground, or
subtract paces if the leg is downhill.

If you use pace counting frequently, it is a good idea to stick a
home-made pacing scale on to the side of your compass. This is placed
on the map next to the distance that is to be run. Gradations on the
scale tell you how many paces you will need, cutting down on the
amount of mental arithmetic required.

A different pacing scale has to be made for each map scale. If you use
40 double paces to cover 100m, and the map scale is 1:15 000, then
ten double paces will cover 25m, or about 1.7mm on the map. At a
scale of 1:10 000 this distance would be 2.5mm on the map.

Pace counting may occasionally provide the key to finding a difficult
control. On the other hand, it should be remembered that pace counting is unreliable or impossible on very steep or rough ground.

## Using judgement and feel

With practice, it is possible to become skilled at recognizing distances
on the ground. Some people are able to look ahead and identify a feature that they judge to be, say, 50m away (it helps if you are, say, a
cricketer who knows that a wicket is 20m long, or a track athlete who
knows that a finishing straight is about 100m long). If you want to

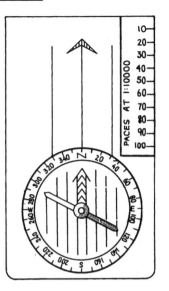

**6.2** A home-made pacing scale for an orienteer who uses 30 paces per 100m, for use with a 1:10 000 map. Each gradation is for 10 paces, or 33m, which is 3.3mm at 1:10 000.

cover 300m then you will have to split this into several sections of perhaps 50m, depending on how far you can see across the terrain.

In reality, many successful orienteers estimate distance purely by feel: they just keep running until they feel they have gone far enough. To do this well obviously requires a great deal of practice; it is essential to develop a feel for the map scale you are using, and this is only achieved through experience. The advantage of going by feel is that it leaves your head uncluttered with numbers, so that you are free to concentrate on reading the map detail, using the compass, and, just as importantly, enjoying the orienteering. Having said this, if you choose to judge distance by feel it is still well worth knowing how to pace count, just in case you ever encounter an exceptionally difficult control.

Distance estimation can sometimes be used together with an accurate compass bearing in a technique known as 'aiming-off'. In this situation orienteers deliberately aim to one side of the feature they are hoping to find. When they judge that they have gone far enough they then know which way to turn. An example of this is shown in figure 6.1.

# 7

# Understanding contours

Using contours is the key to successful navigation. Experienced orienteers use contours more than any other feature when they are map-reading, because contours show the ground as a complete picture, depicting both the overall layout of the main hills and valleys, and the intricacies of areas of smaller features. In addition, contour features never change with time, unlike tracks, paths and vegetation boundaries which are frequently altered by forestry activity.

Unfortunately, contours are the hardest part of the map to understand, as they require you to imagine a three-dimensional landscape in your head, based on the brown squiggles on a flat piece of paper.

## What are contours?

A contour is an imaginary line joining points of equal height, so a series of contours will show the shape and steepness of the ground.

Orienteering maps usually use a contour interval of 5m; in other words, as you climb a hill you will cross a contour line with every 5m of vertical height that you gain. A hill which is about 5m high (roughly the height of two storeys of a building) will only have one contour around it. Contours are sometimes mapped at an interval of 2.5m, usually when the terrain is flattish but very detailed, for instance in coastal sand-dune areas.

In orienteering jargon, small valleys are usually referred to as 're-entrants', small ridges as 'spurs' and passes between two small hills as 'saddles' or 'cols'.

## What is up and what is down?

One of the first things you need to do when assessing any given leg on an orienteering course is to work out the overall shape of the ground.

It is important to distinguish the ridges from the valleys. Valleys, of course, usually contain water features such as rivers, streams, marshes or lakes, and this is a useful guide, except in country where water

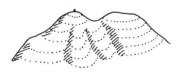

(a) Two hills as they would appear with contours superimposed

(b) The same two hills represented by contours on the map

**7.1** Contours.

features are rare. Hills are encircled by closed contour lines, and the tags on crags always point downhill. In valleys the contours always point upstream, and on ridges the contours point downhill. Every fifth contour on the map will be drawn with a thicker line. These 'index contours' help to make the overall shape of the land stand out on the map. Generally, once you have sorted out one part of the map, the rest will quickly make sense, but take care not to make the mistake of inverting the relief: in other words, seeing all the ups as downs, and vice versa.

When you look at the fine detail on the map, for instance when you are trying to interpret the small features around a control, it can also be difficult to work out what is up and what is down. Where the contours are hard to understand, the mapper will add small 'tags' to the contour lines; these point downhill. Closed contour lines not only encircle hills, they can also depict hollows or depressions, and these are always drawn with tags pointing inwards, or downhill (see figure 7.1). Tags are not usually drawn on knolls, but when they are they point outwards.

Some small features lie between the levels of two contours and so cannot be shown with a 5m contour line. The mapper may show these by adding a short section of extra contour line known as a 'form line'. These are drawn as dashed brown lines on the map.

## Contour features as handrails

You can follow linear contour features in the same way as following paths, fences, streams and so on. Linear contour features may include long, narrow knolls or depressions, or ridges and re-entrants.

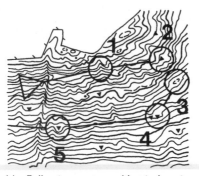 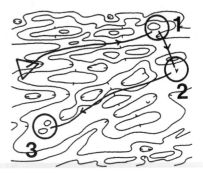

(a) Following contours (that is, keeping to the same level) or crossing them at an angle is a useful aid to navigation

(b) Linear contour feature such as ridges, valleys, knolls and long hollows can all be followed to simplify navigation

**7.2** Using contours (a) on a slope, and (b) as handrails.

 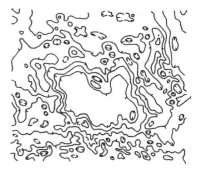

(a) Intricate terrain: complex, knolly contours from Torver Common in Cumbria, England

(b) Difficult sand-dune terrain, with many small knolls and depressions, from a New Zealand orienteering map

**7.3** Two examples of intricate contour detail.

The contours on a steep, smooth slope can be used to simplify navigation. For example: if you are running between two features on the same contour line then you know that you just have to stick to the same level. Alternatively, you may have to cross the contour lines at right angles, in other words directly up or down the slope.

## Dealing with intricate contour detail

In certain types of terrain the ground shapes are especially complex. These areas provide challenging orienteering as they test the orienteer's ability to use contours for navigation.

Scandinavian forests contain particularly rocky, broken ground with numerous small knolls, lakes and marshes. Similar 'Nordic' ground shapes occur in British upland areas in North Wales, the Lake District and Scotland, as well as in the forests of New England in the United States. Sand-dune areas also contain very intricate contour detail in the form of a chaotic mass of small ridges, knolls and depressions (see Chapter 11).

It helps to simplify areas of complex contour detail by looking for the major features. There may well be larger ridges and valleys that stand out from the smaller features, while sand-dune areas are often arranged into long, snaking ridges separated by wide, flat areas of low ground. These features can be followed like handrails or, if you are crossing the grain of the land, can be ticked off as you pass them.

It is not a good idea, however, to simplify contour detail when you are near a control. Instead, it is important to try to understand everything on the map around the control site. With practice, contours can be used to form an excellent mental picture of the ground (see Chapter 5). In fact, when forming a mental picture the contours should be the first things you look at, for instance the patterns of the re-entrants and knolls around the control. Then you should imagine how the other features such as crags and marshes fit into the contour picture. Rather than

**7.4** Visualization using contours. The orienteer has formed a mental picture of the terrain around the control site from the contours on the map.

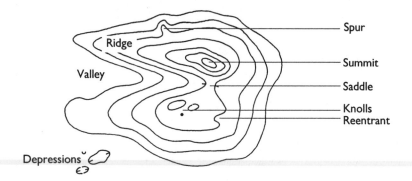

**7.5** Features depicted by contours.

just saying, for example, 'I will pass a crag, then a boulder', you should say, 'There will be a knoll with a crag on the side of it, then a re-entrant containing a boulder.'

## Practising using contours

The best way to understand contours is to walk around in a complex, well-mapped area. Look at the way in which contour features are shown: they are often exaggerated by the mapper in order to make them stand out and to make them look right to the runner. Try to get a feel for the standard 5m contour interval. How big is a one-contour knoll compared to a two-contour knoll? When is a knoll too small to be shown with a contour, and is shown instead with a brown dot symbol? Knolls drawn with form lines may be quite low – only a metre or so higher than the surrounding ground.

Look at the way in which contours are drawn closer together as the ground gets steeper. Knolls and re-entrants all have their own individual shapes, which are shown on the map. On a slope, the contours show the relative levels of different features. Terraces and flat areas should stand out in hilly terrain, and these are often just as helpful to the map reader as are knolls and ridges.

It takes a lot of practice to learn how to use contours well, but in the long run it is worth it. Some experienced orienteers do everything they can to avoid using contours. Instead, they try to rely on other features, and on compass and pace counting, but ultimately this approach limits their success as map-readers. It is better to keep trying to use contours, even if you have problems to start with.

# 8

## Route choice

Very often there is no problem in choosing the best route between two controls. It may be obvious; along a path, say, or perhaps a straight line through flat, open forest. On some legs, however, there may a number of different options to consider. Course planners deliberately try to set legs involving route choice, as this adds an extra dimension to the orienteering.

---

### Factors to consider when choosing a route:

---

- How far you have to run on each route. The straight line route is obviously the shortest in terms of distance. Detours may provide faster running, but you will end up covering more ground.
- The amount of climbing on each route. Climbing hills is both time-consuming and hard work! It may be worth making a large detour to avoid crossing ridges and valleys.
- Steep slopes. If you have to climb a hill it may be better to make a gradual, slanting ascent than to take the steepest line.
- Path routes. Path and road routes are both faster running and easier to follow than routes through terrain. It is often worth running extra distance in order to follow paths.
- Things that get in the way! These include 'green areas' (dense vegetation shown as green on the map), marshes, rocky ground, felled areas – in fact anything that slows you down that you may decide to avoid. Some features, such as lakes or high crags, leave you no option but to find a way round.
- Safe routes. If you are a beginner it may be worth looking for a safe route that enables you to follow line features and provides a good attack point from which to approach the control. Top competitors in the 'elite' categories almost always take the fastest route even if it is the most difficult to follow, relying on their technical ability to keep them on course.

---

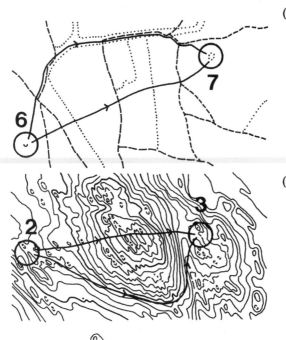

(a) Straight or around the paths? The path route is longer, but offers faster running and easier navigation

(b) Over or round? The direct route involves climbing a large hill

(c) Safe or risky? The southern route provides a good attack point from which to approach the control, while the straight route may appeal to the confident orienteer

**8.1** Factors in route choice.

## Reaching a decision

It helps to have a routine to go through when you are assessing possible route choice options. Here is a list of actions that may help you to reach the right decision:

• First decide if there is any reason why you should not run straight. If there is nothing in the way and there is no faster option, then set off along the straight line – there is no need for any further thought! If you cannot go straight, then continue with this list.

- Take a general overview of the whole leg, trying to obtain an overall picture of the ground in one go. Very often a logical line will present itself.
- Check that you have not missed a good route by looking at every possible option, even those that seem unlikely at first. It is a common mistake to view legs with 'tunnel vision', missing routes that make a large detour from the straight line.
- If you cannot decide between two routes, then there is probably little between them anyway. Choose one and get on with it!
- When you have chosen a route, stick to it with conviction – it is often a mistake to change your mind half-way along the leg. Forget about the merits of other routes and concentrate on the navigation required to follow the route you have chosen.

It is often the case that no one manages to choose all the best routes, not even the winner. The main thing is to select routes that are all reasonable without making any major route choice errors.

## Counting contours

This technique gives you a rough idea of how much climb there is on different options. It is quickest to count just the index contours – the thicker lines on the map – counting only those contours you will cross when you are going uphill. This all takes some time, so it is only worth doing if you are very unsure and you think you may be heavily penalized by choosing the wrong route. Some types of terrain present particularly mind-boggling route-choice problems, for instance the very hilly forests of the Swiss Alps, which often contain a bewildering mass of steep ridges and valleys.

## Estimating route lengths

As a rough rule of thumb, the width of the gap between your route and the straight line is equivalent to the extra distance of your route. Therefore the relative distances of routes can be judged by seeing how far they depart from the straight line, assuming that they follow a fairly smooth curve. It has been said that an extra 10m of climbing is equivalent, timewise, to an extra 100m of level running. If you are very good at doing sums in your head then you may be able to use this formula in combination with counting contours, but otherwise forget it! There can be so many factors involved in choosing a route that it is often

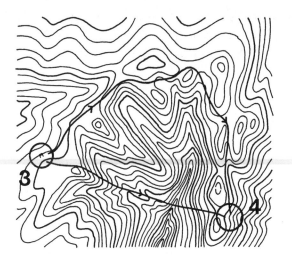

**8.2** Counting contours and estimating distance. The straight route climbs an extra two index contours, but the flatter route around the ridge is about 300m further. Which would you choose?

better to make a judgement based on gut feeling rather than on calculation. It helps to have plenty of experience, plus a knowledge of the kind of terrain you are running in.

## Planning ahead

Choosing a route can take some time. Rather than standing at a control working out how to do the next leg, it is better to have the leg sorted out in advance. If you find yourself walking up a hill early in the course then this is a good opportunity to plan ahead, as it is easier to read the map when you are not moving fast. Look at the rest of the course to see if there is a route choice leg, and make a mental note of the best route. You may still need to stop at the control at the beginning of the leg to double-check, but this is still much quicker than making a decision from scratch.

## Route-choice tactics

If you are preparing for an event that you are particularly keen to do well in, and are familiar with the kind of terrain you will be running in, it may be worth working out a plan to help you with route choice legs. For example: you may decide to take path routes ('going round is sound!'), because you expect the terrain to be slow going. Or you may decide that 'straight is great' and keep to the straight line between controls. In certain very sandy or muddy areas the paths may in fact be slower than the terrain. You may decide to avoid climbing hills wherever possible – perhaps because you know that the course will be longer than you are used to and you want to save energy. In some terrains it may be better to follow lines of marshes in order to keep to flatter ground, while in others the marshes may be overgrown and the ridge tops therefore faster. Even if you are unfamiliar with the terrain before the event, you may be able to form an impression during the first few legs which will help you to choose routes later on.

Having said this, it always pays to keep an open mind and not to follow a pre-determined plan blindly. In some areas there is no one rule as to which route is best. Each leg should be judged on its own merits.

# 9

# Advanced techniques

Orienteering techniques can be divided into two categories: 'rough orienteering' and 'fine orienteering'. Rough-Orienteering skills are used during the first part of a leg, when the aim is to cover the ground as fast as possible. Fine-orienteering skills are used to find the control at the end of the leg.

## Rough orienteering

The aim of rough orienteering is to navigate quickly and reasonably accurately. It is especially useful on longer legs, where you are trying to get somewhere close to the next control without wasting any time. It is a difficult skill to perfect, as it involves finding a balance between speed and caution. A very common error is to be over-cautious on long legs and to try to read too much map detail.

### *Rough compass*

The compass is very important in rough orienteering. If you are good at running straight with the compass you will be able to ignore a lot of map detail, and hence save time. Even if you completely lose track of your position, you should be able to keep going at full speed, confident in your bearing, and then relocate later on without wasting time (see page 59). You can use the compass in any of the three ways described in Chapter 5 to keep the map set, take a bearing or run on the needle. It does not really matter exactly how you use the compass, as long as you use it well.

During rough orienteering, it helps to be able to set the compass and to follow bearings without stopping running. This takes a bit of practice: take care not to trip over or run into any trees while you are perfecting the skill! As mentioned on page 34, you should use the compass to take sightings on features in the distance, rather than follow the needle itself.

## *Rough map-reading*

The map-reading side of rough orienteering involves simplifying features in order to save time. If you are running through an area of complex contour detail, you need only be aware of the major ridges and valleys that you will cross; to read every tiny bump and hollow would waste time. Alternatively, you may be able to follow a natural line around the larger hills and through obvious saddles. Similarly, if you are following paths there is no need to read every feature that you see at the side of the path. It takes practice to know just how far to simplify things – rough orienteering could be described as 'the art of knowing just how much you can get away with'.

Rough orienteering involves both 'map-to-ground' and 'ground-to-map' skills. Map-to-ground means looking at the map and forming a mental picture, and then fitting this to the features that you see on the ground when you are running. Ground-to-map means running over the ground until you see a distinctive feature, and then identifying it on the map. The mental picture that you form during map-to-ground should be simplified, including only those features that are necessary to keep you on course and to tell you how far you have gone. The ground-to-map side is useful, as it helps you to pinpoint your position now and then without using up much time. It is also essential in mid-leg relocation (see page 59).

# Fine orienteering

The aim of fine orienteering is simply to find the control at the end of the leg. It is therefore only used during the last 100–200m of the leg. Here, it is relatively unimportant to be fast: accuracy is the main priority. You should use every technique at your disposal – compass, map-reading and distance estimation.

Somewhere along the leg there will be a transition from rough to fine orienteering. This may be at a large, easily recognized feature, or 'attack point'; alternatively, the transition may be gradual. Some orienteers prefer a disciplined approach involving a carefully chosen attack point, while others never think in terms of attack points but instead slow down gradually on the approach to the control. If you are a beginner, it is a good idea to start off using definite attack points.

## *Fine compass*

The compass is always important in fine orienteering. If there is plenty of detail on the map, then it should be used as a back-up to map-

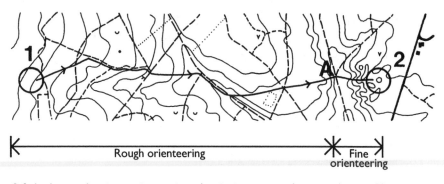

K—————————— Rough orienteering ——————————✕— Fine ⟩|
                                                   orienteering

**9.1** In the rough-orienteering section, the aim is to cover the ground as quickly as possible using rough compass and by 'ticking off' the larger features, such as major tracks and valleys. In this example, the orienteer has chosen an attack point at A, from which to begin a final approach to the control using careful, accurate, fine-orienteering techniques.

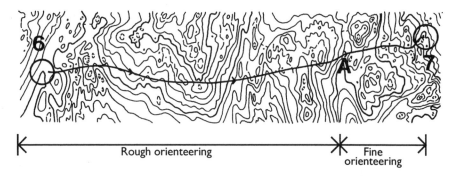

K—————————— Rough orienteering ——————————✕— Fine ⟩|
                                                   orienteering

**9.2** In this contour example, the orienteer has simplified the rough orienteering by taking note of only the major valleys, ridges and summits. After the attack point at A, he has taken care to follow every feature into the control, using 'continuous-contact' orienteering. The simplified map below represents the map information taken in by the runner at different stages of the leg.

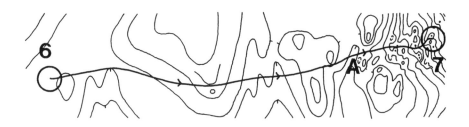

reading. In this situation it can be used to set the map or for taking a bearing. If there is little detail on the map the compass becomes even more important, and it is usually wise to take an accurate bearing.

To use the compass very accurately, hold it as level and as steady as possible when taking sightings; it is worth standing still for a second or two in order to do this, in contrast to rough orienteering when the compass can be used without stopping running. It is also worth using distance estimation when there is little detail on the map, either by pace counting or judgement (see Chapter 6).

### Fine map-reading: visualization

Before approaching a control it is vital to have a good mental picture of all the features on the way in to it, as well as to either side and beyond. Unlike rough map-reading, it is unwise to simplify the detail. You should be using 'map-to-ground' rather than 'ground-to-map'.

Try to visualize where the control will be situated relative to other features – especially the contour features, if any. You may need to refer to the control description sheet to find out exactly which feature the marker is sited on: very many mistakes are made by rushing into the area of the control with a poor mental picture of the ground. Once you have a clear picture, then try to 'tick off' every feature as you pass it. This is sometimes referred to as 'continuous contact' orienteering.

## Putting it together

On the majority of legs it is appropriate to use the method described above; that is, fast, rough orienteering to an attack point, then careful fine orienteering to the control. There are some exceptions to this rule, however. On certain legs the hardest navigation, where you need to use fine-orienteering skills, may come in the middle of the leg rather than at the end; for example, it may be vital to pick up a small path, footbridge, or pass between two hills. On other legs the control site may in fact be quite easy, so to slow down and use careful, fine navigation would be a waste of time. It is therefore best to be flexible in the way you use rough and fine orienteering.

## Speed control

As orienteers improve and gain experience they tend to become less reliant on a distinct attack point, instead constantly varying their speed to allow for the difficulties imposed by the navigation. A world champion from Norway once said, 'The hardest part of orienteering is knowing how fast to run.' Although he was probably running flat out for most of the course, there were just a few key moments – perhaps one or two on each leg – when he realized that it was essential to put the brakes on and take particular care.

## Planning ahead

In order to control your speed well, you will need to plan ahead by looking at the next part of the course in order to identify difficult sections. Before you start each leg, it is important always to have a clear plan and to know which route you will follow, where the hard parts are and what techniques you will use, rather than just setting off and seeing what happens. In addition, it is useful to have a rough idea of what the next few legs hold in store.

The best time to plan ahead is when you are walking up a steep hill: it is easier to read the map when you are moving slowly. You can also plan ahead when you have a long run along a path or road: the smoother surface makes it easier to read the map on the run, and there is no need to think about the immediate navigation. Some orienteers complain that running along tracks is tedious and call it 'dead-running' – this perhaps shows that they are guilty of not making full use of this 'free time' to look at the rest of the course and plan ahead.

---

### Things to look for when planning ahead:

---

- Route choice legs – try to spot these in advance and roughly work out the best route so that you do not spend too long standing still at the control at the start of the leg.
- Difficult controls – these might be features sited in areas of confusingly complex detail, or small features in otherwise featureless terrain. Anything in dense, low-visibility forest is likely to be tricky, while approaching controls diagonally across steep slopes also requires care. Make a mental note of the difficult controls and decide in advance which fine-orienteering techniques you will use to find them.
- Sections of the course in technically difficult terrain – course planners frequently set a series of short legs in the hardest part of the area. It helps to be ready for these in advance, so that they do not come as too much of a shock.
- How the terrain changes around the course – in Great Britain, for example, it is common for the course to cross several distinctly

different types of terrain, perhaps from forest on to open moorland and then back into forest. In this situation you will need to slow down when going back into the forest where the visibility is much lower.

- The general layout of the course, especially where the big climbs are – it helps psychologically to know what lies ahead as you will feel more in control. In hilly regions, orienteering courses are often 'a race of two halves', climbing for the first half and descending for the second. It helps if you can say to yourself, 'Keep going, it's all downhill soon!'

## Control flow

If you have good control flow, you will be able to run into a control, punch your control card, and then run off to the next control smoothly and quickly. Control flow only saves a few seconds at each control, but over a course with perhaps 20 controls these seconds can easily add up to minutes. Control flow is therefore a way in which experienced orienteers can save small amounts of time; for the less experienced, it is more important to concentrate on improving map and compass skills – control flow only really saves time if you have already mastered the art of map-reading on the run.

It is a good idea to have an automatic routine at controls, which you go through without thinking – so that it does not distract from the other aspects of the orienteering. Control flow is easy to practise, so at your next event try to concentrate on the routine below.

### Control flow routine:

- Always know which route you will take on the next leg before reaching the control. That way, you will be able to avoid standing still.
- Always know the control code and description before you get there, although if the feature is obvious from the map then do not bother reading the description.
- After you have spotted the control feature, but before you reach it, try to see the line in the terrain that you are going to take on the way out.
- Punch your card quickly and leave the marker straightaway.

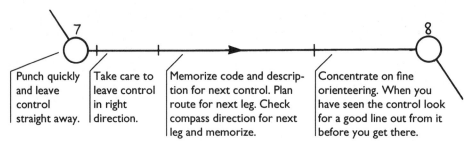

| Punch quickly and leave control straight away. | Take care to leave control in right direction. | Memorize code and description for next control. Plan route for next leg. Check compass direction for next leg and memorize. | Concentrate on fine orienteering. When you have seen the control look for a good line out from it before you get there. |

**9.3** Control flow and planning ahead.

## *Punching quickly*

It helps if you carry your control card so that it is easily accessible for punching; the best methods are either to pin the card to a wrist band or to attach it to a wrist loop. It is easier to get the card in and out of the punch if it is stiffened with tape or clear adhesive plastic. Punches are usually either hung on strings or nailed horizontally to trestles, so it is worthwhile practising punching at both of these. If you write the control codes and descriptions into the boxes on your card, it is easy to read and memorize them while running. Then as you are running into the control, get your card ready to punch. As you punch, keep your thumb on your position on the map, otherwise you will be fumbling around refinding your position at every control. For this reason, it is not such a good idea to hold the map in your mouth while punching the card.

As well as saving seconds, control flow helps you to orienteer more smoothly and stylishly. It is better psychologically to be fluent and in control of things, rather than to arrive at the control with map, compass and control card tangled, and then have to stand still to think about the route on the next leg. In fact, many experienced orienteers say that if their control flow starts to break down it is often the first sign that they are getting tired and losing concentration, and may be heading for a navigational mistake unless they can make an effort to get things under control once more.

## Relocation: what to do when you get lost

Getting lost can be an unpleasant experience. Things seem to be going well for a while, until you gradually become aware that the map does not quite match the ground. You know you are near the control, but you do not know which way to turn... and all the time the clock is ticking on and a growing feeling of panic and frustration makes it hard to keep a clear head. In this situation – familiar to all orienteers – it does help to have a ready-made plan of action. Certainly any positive strategy is better than running around aimlessly.

Relocation is a skill in its own right. The best orienteers lose track of their position surprisingly often, but many are able to relocate so quickly that their mistakes cost them seconds rather than minutes. This section explains the two different types of relocation. The first is useful when you are lost in the middle of a leg, the second when you are somewhere close to the control.

## *Mid-leg relocation*

This technique is useful if you are running a longish leg on a straight-line route: in other words, if you are following the compass, ticking off features as you pass them. When you are in this situation and find that you have lost track of your position, and that the features on the map do not fit those on the ground, it is usually best to keep going without slowing down, relying on the compass to keep you on course. With any luck, you will soon reach a feature that you can identify on the map. To stop straightaway in order to relocate would waste time unnec-

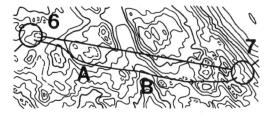

(a) In this example, the orienteer lost track of his position during the first part of the leg, at A. However, he was confident in his compass and knew that he would reach the major re-entrant at B, so he continued on his original course without slowing down.

**9.4** Relocation
(a) in mid-leg, and (b) near the control.

(b) In this example, the runner became confused by the many small knolls near the control. As she could not identify any easily recognizable features she headed straight on to the path where she relocated on the path bend. By acting quickly and decisively she was able to cut her losses to one or two minutes.

essarily. In certain types of terrain, for instance in parts of Scandinavia where the ground is detailed and the best route is usually straight, it is fairly commonplace to lose track of your position in mid-leg, but if you are confident in your compass and in your ability to relocate, there is no reason why you should lose any time as a result.

If you are lost in mid-leg but are not following a straight-line route, then it may be better to stop in order to relocate. When you have stopped, the first thing to do is to set the map with the compass, as this makes it much easier to match the features around you to the map. If you still cannot relocate, then there is no option but to move on in what you feel to be the right direction until you see a feature that is recognizable on the map. Alternatively, you may decide to head out to a large, obvious feature such as a road or lake where you will be sure of your position. Once at this feature, replan your route to the control from your new position. Do not rush in order to make up lost time – a common mistake – or you could end up getting lost all over again!

## Relocation near the control

If you are lost somewhere close to the control, the first thing to do is to set the map with the compass, in order to fit the features around you to the map. You may have to move around in order to find some distinctive looking features. If you have spent several minutes trying to do this without any luck, then the best plan is to head out to a large feature such as a line feature in order to relocate. Keep your eyes open when you are heading out, as you may see some smaller distinctive feature on the way there. You might even bump into your control! If there are no nearby line features on which to relocate, you could consider retracing your steps the way you came until you know where you are. Again, once you have relocated, replan your route to the control, take a new bearing and do not rush to make up lost time. If the control was hard the first time round it will probably still be hard on the second.

## Fitting the map to the ground

The ability to do this quickly is the fundamental skill of relocation, and can only really be improved with practice. The ease with which you can match the map to the ground is closely related to your skill as a map-reader. Like map-reading, the only way to get better is to spend as much time as possible running in detailed, well-mapped terrain. Some training exercises aimed at improving relocation are described in Chapter 11.

# The psychology of racing

Some of the most successful orienteers have made it to the top despite lacking the fitness and technical flair of their rivals. Other superbly fit and technically gifted competitors never quite manage to live up to their potential. This is due to a third and vital aspect to orienteering beyond fitness and technique, and that is the ability to race well: in other words, to get the very best out of yourself on the day of a big race. Racing ability is closely linked to psychology, and good racers tend be strong in concentration, self-confidence and motivation.

These factors are all related to one another. Motivation, or the desire to win, is what fuels the intense concentration required to get around a long, tough course without making any mistakes. Motivation also drives good racers to run to the limits of their physical ability when other runners are tempted to take it easy. Self-confidence is also vital to success: anyone who believes that they are the best is already half-way towards winning. These psychological factors are to a large extent built into the runner's own personality. It is difficult, although not impossible, to develop and change them in order to race better. The methods described below can help in overcoming psychological problems.

## Following a routine

Some runners claim that they make mistakes as a result of being too nervous. To remedy this, they refuse to take any event too seriously and therefore never quite run to their full potential. A better solution would be to learn to control their nerves more effectively. Most elite competitors go through a pre-race routine which has a calming effect, partly because it keeps them busy, and partly because it feels familiar and reassuring. This routine might include getting changed, preparing equipment, warming up and stretching.

## Setting goals

A lack of motivation, in some ways the opposite of the situation described above, can be improved by setting personal goals. Having trained and aimed for a race for several months, there is usually no problem in getting fired up on the day of the race.

## Avoiding early mistakes

Many orienteers will consistently make a bad mistake during the first few legs of a course, and then run cleanly to the finish. This shows that they are running too fast at the start of the course, perhaps due to nervousness. The best way around this is to approach the first few legs of a race very carefully, so that there is little chance of going wrong. By then you will have settled into the course and the freshness will have gone from your legs.

## Getting out of a 'bad patch'

Most orienteers go through the occasional bad patch, when every race seems to be a disaster. After a couple of bad runs, they start expecting to make mistakes and begin to lose self-confidence; they then cannot concentrate fully on the navigation, because part of their mind is always worrying about the next mistake, resulting in more and more bad runs. The way out of this vicious circle is to slow right down in the next race, almost to walking pace if necessary, and make absolutely certain that everything goes perfectly. This not only solves the psychological problem, but provides a chance to return to the basics of map and compass in case there is also an underlying technical problem involved.

---

### Some common mistakes:

---

- The 180° error – everyone does this sooner or later! It is caused by setting the compass 'the wrong way round': in other words, with the baseplate round the wrong way when you take the bearing from the map, so that you run in exactly the opposite direction when you are following the bearing.
- The parallel error – a common map-reading error, made by thinking you are following a feature or set of features when you are in fact following another, similar feature. It is easy to convince yourself that you are in the right place and to make the map fit the ground, especially when you do not want to accept that you have gone wrong. Parallel errors can be the result of not using the compass as a back-up to map-reading: the compass would soon show that the features were not running in quite the right direction. It also helps to keep on the lookout for situations where it is possible to make a parallel error and to take extra care accordingly.
- Compass errors – ignoring the compass in favour of the map is the cause of the majority of mistakes. The compass is *always* right, whereas the map can be misleading. In the map example, the orienteer has followed a hillside at the wrong level and has been pulled on to the wrong course. A quick check of the compass would have shown that something was wrong.

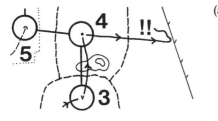

(a) Every orienteer makes this disastrous mistake at one time or another! It is caused either by setting the compass with the baseplate misplaced on the map by 180°, or by following the south needle on the compass rather than the north

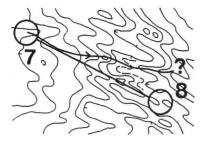

(b) In this example, the orienteer has followed the wrong set of features for a considerable distance, instead of taking care to pick up the right ridge, using accurate compass, earlier in the leg

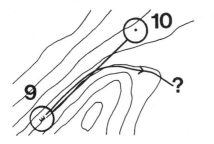

(c) Here, the orienteer has ignored the compass and tried to follow the slope into the control. Unfortunately, he was running at the wrong level and was misled by the curve of the hillside

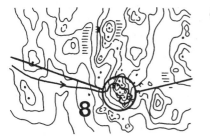

(d) The orienteer has run into the control circle without forming a mental picture of the shape of the ground and the relative positions of features. They had also failed to look at the control description to clarify the exact location of the marker.

**9.5** Common mistakes: (a) the 180° error; (b) the parallel error; (c) the compass error; (d) the error in the control circle caused by poor visualization of the features around the control site.

- Following – this is a real-life example described by a runner on the first loop of a World Championships Relay: 'I followed a group of runners who were in fact heading for a different first control. When we got there, it had the wrong code letters. It took me a couple of minutes to work out where I was, then a minute or so to get to the right control. By this time the other runners were well ahead and I had no chance of catching them.' Other runners can be a help, but it is important not to follow them blindly. It is best to concentrate on your own orienteering, at the same time keeping an eye on what everyone else is doing.
- An error 'in the circle' – most errors in the control circle are due to poor visualization of the features around the control site, often due to rushing in without slowing down.

---

## *Steve's Week; 1993 World Orienteering Championships,* NEW YORK STATE

During the fall, the forests of New York State are an orienteer's paradise, a rocky wilderness with few paths or signs of human settlement. The terrain is complex and challenging, a mixture of intricate craggy knolls, thickets of mountain laurel and sinister-looking, waterlogged swamps. The weather at this time of year is perfect for running: pale blue skies, a crisp frost in the morning, and then warm sunshine later in the day. From the highest parts of the forest, where the hills break through the tree cover, such as at the summit of Bear Mountain by the Hudson River, it is possible to see for miles through the clear air, over an undulating expanse of trees and lakes, to the distant spires and towers of Manhattan. All this wilderness, apparently forgotten since the days of the last of the Mohicans, is only hours from the Big Apple.

Steve Hale travelled to New York as part of a well-prepared, confident British team. Both Steve and fellow team member Yvette Hague were ranked in the top five in the world and were pursuing the same elusive dream: a World Championship medal. Up until then, orienteering had been dominated by a handful of nations – the Scandinavians, Czechs and Swiss. The British, in common with other teams such as the Australians, New Zealanders, French, Hungarians, Russians, Estonians and Latvians, had tried hard for years to make a breakthrough and challenge the top countries, yet had still failed to escape from the 'second division'. No Briton had ever won a World Championship medal.

Steve and Yvette were typical of a group of stars emerging from the so-called B Nations – countries where the sport is relatively new. They were part of the first generation of runners to have grown up with the sport from childhood, both having started orienteering before the age of ten. In their middle to late twenties they had built up a level of fitness, technique and experience to challenge seriously the top Scandinavians. Steve's physical training, totalling as much as 16 hours of running each week, was equivalent to that of any international marathon runner, and, like many top orienteers, he was also able to compete at the highest levels as a road and cross-country runner.

The first event of the championships was the Short Distance Race. A winning time of just 25 minutes means that many competitors can maintain a very high running speed throughout the course, but it is easy to run too fast, beyond one's technical limits, and to make mistakes as a result. The finishing times are so close that the smallest error can prove costly, so it is vital to have good speed control and a razor-sharp technique. Control flow is important, as is the ability to shut out all external pressure and concentrate fully on the orienteering.

Steve's pre-race advice to his fellow team members had been simple: 'Don't rush!' Other team members recalled the maxim of Carol McNeill, up until then Britain's most successful World Championship runner, with a seventh place in 1979: 'Don't think about running fast, think about orienteering fast.'

Steve's supporters at the finish saw him storm down the run-in to record the equal fastest time of the day, but then, in a nail-biting finale, were disappointed to watch three later starters cross the line in marginally quicker times. Steve's final position was equal fourth, missing a medal by only one second. He had achieved the best ever placing by a Briton in a World Championships, and had gone some way towards putting British orienteering on the map, yet had failed win a medal by the narrowest possible margin.

Two days later, in the Classic Distance Race, Yvette went one better, finishing in bronze medal position behind runners from Sweden and Finland. Steve's own race fell apart at the seventh control, where a huge eight-minute mistake caused him to plummet from third to forty-sixth position; it is virtually impossible to recover from a mistake of more than three minutes at world-class level. His bitter disappointment was deepened by the knowledge that the mistake was entirely his own fault, as in the space of a few minutes he had managed to neglect several of the basic principles of navigation. His initial error was caused by being misled by similar contour features and veering off course by 90°. At this stage, he would normally have expected to return to the correct line with the loss of only a few seconds, following a routine glance at the compass (a fairly normal occurrence at this standard of competition), but he failed to back up his map-reading with the compass and compounded the parallel error by mistakenly crossing the wrong marsh and climbing on to the wrong hill. Even at this stage Steve would normally have expected to relocate within a minute or two, but it was a further five or six minutes before he was able to identify a distinctive feature and continue more carefully to the control. For a competitor of his ability and experience, such an uncharacteristic series of errors suggests that the underlying cause may have been psychological. Perhaps he had been tempted into abandoning his 'don't rush' tactics of the Short Distance Race, in the knowledge that every extra second gained would increase his prospects of a medal. There was also the pressure of knowing that it was 'now or never' – Steve was in top form, the terrain suited him and the next World Championships was a distant two years away. There was also an element of misfortune in his mistake. The 90-minute Classic Distance Race is a test of concentration and stamina as much as anything, and everyone goes through periods where their attention wanders. Many people get away with it, but Steve was unlucky.

The final race was the Relay Competition. As the culmination to an amazing roller-coaster week of success and failure, delight and disappointment, Steve produced one of the most remarkable runs of any World Championships. He was to run the fourth and final loop for the British team. After two loops the team were lying in tenth position. Then an aggressive and technically perfect run from the third-loop runner, Stephen Palmer, pulled the team up to fifth position; his time was later confirmed as the third fastest of the day. Stephen handed over to Steve, who was still faced with an almost impossible task. He was six minutes behind the leaders, Switzerland, and was aiming to catch several of the best runners in the world. Hot on his heels, in sixth and seventh positions, were the two newly crowned World Champions: Peter Thoresen from Norway, winner of the Short Race, and Alan Mogensen from Denmark, winner of the Classic Distance Race.

Steve, however, had no thoughts for the runners behind him – his sights were firmly set on the teams in front. He had two minutes to catch up on the Russian and Swedish runners, and passed them early in the course to move into third position. He was now fired up and flying through the forest, and eventually pulled back a further three minutes to pass the Finnish runner in second place. As he crossed the finish line he was just 15 seconds behind the leading Swiss athlete. In Steve's words: 'Another kilometre and I'd have got him!' He had managed to bring the British team home in silver medal position thanks to a spectacular, flawless piece of orienteering. His time for the 10.2km loop was 49.25 minutes, two minutes faster than any other runner. At less than 5 minutes per kilometre, he had covered the tough, rocky terrain at a faster pace than most elite orienteers would dream of achieving on a level parkland course. Together with Yvette Hague in the Classic Distance Race and Stephen Palmer, the British third-loop runner, Steve had helped make a breakthrough the young orienteering nations and many others had been working towards for years. Orienteering had entered a new era.

Steve's performance was the result of a high level of fitness combined with the perfect application of orienteering techniques: rough navigation using map and compass on the run, together with simplifying terrain shapes to save time; speed control, including being aware of exactly the right places to slow down; and fine-orienteering skills, involving more accurate compass and continuous-contact map-reading. Above all, he had achieved a perfect state of mind, confident and yet never outrunning his technique, positive and aiming for the best result he could manage rather than thinking about what might happen if things went wrong. This approach brings rewards at every level of the sport, from beginners, through club orienteers, to World Championship competitors alike.

# 10

# Fitness training for orienteering

## Training to improve

A newcomer to orienteering will improve rapidly simply by taking part in competitions and gaining experience of how events are run, what is shown on the map, using basic techniques, and so on. This improvement will gradually slow down, until a point is reached where the only way to continue to get better is to do some training in addition to running in competitions. Many orienteers are content to remain at a reasonable level and feel no need to train, whereas others, who are perhaps more ambitious and have set themselves higher goals, or maybe have more time at their disposal, are keen to get out and train in order to improve their orienteering. It is important to many people to keep improving, simply because one of the pleasures of taking part in any sport is the thrill that comes from getting better and learning new skills. However, there is certainly no need to train in order to enjoy orienteering – it all depends on how motivated you are and on the level of your personal aspirations.

There are two ways of improving at orienteering: one is to get fitter and faster as a runner, and the other is to get better at navigating. This chapter explains how to go about getting fitter; from starting out at a low level of fitness through to planning a whole year's training, and gives advice on sports injuries and first aid. Chapter 11 then describes training exercises which can be used to improve the different skills involved in navigation.

## The principle of fitness training

Any physical exercise such as running has the effect of tiring out the body and causing a small degree of wear and tear on all those parts of the body involved in the exercise. The natural response of the body is to recover until it is not only fully repaired, but is stronger than it was before the exercise. Training makes use of this principle to improve gradually the strength and flexibility of the joints and muscles and increase the efficiency of the cardiovascular system (heart and lungs).

The danger of training lies in not allowing the body sufficient time

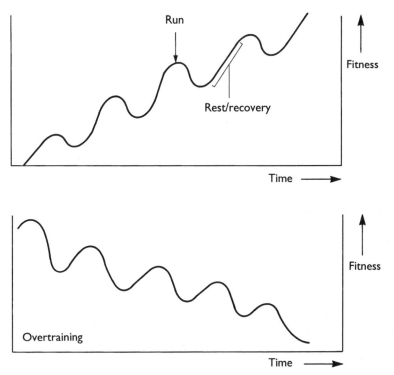

10.1 Principles of fitness training and overtraining.

to recover between sessions. This is known as 'overtraining': the body becomes more and more run down and prone to injury and illness. All physical training therefore has to be planned carefully in order to include sufficient rest and recovery. It is also important to build up the level at which you train very gradually, and to avoid sudden increases in the amount that you do.

## Starting fitness training

If you have never trained before, then any small amount of running or other exercise – perhaps a short jog in midweek or participation in another sport – will have a beneficial effect. If you have never run much in the past but have taken part regularly in other sports, then you may feel able to do a bit more than this. Keep some kind of aim in the back of your mind – something you are trying to achieve as a result of the training. It may be that you want to be able to complete a course without having to slow down and start walking towards the end, or that you want to feel more comfortable while running and thereby enjoy orienteering more, while at the same time having a clearer head to think about the navigation.

It is important to bear in mind the dangers of overtraining as described above.

---

### Dos and don'ts of fitness training

---

- Allow yourself plenty of time to recover between runs.
- Do not suddenly increase the amount you do.
- Do not run if you still feel tired from the last run.
- Listen to what your body is telling you.

---

If all goes well, running will quickly cease to be a shock to the system – an uncomfortable, breathless experience – and will instead seem relatively easy, perhaps even enjoyable!

If you can, try to train on a soft surface such as on grass or woodland paths, as running on surfaced roads and pavements causes repetitive jarring on the legs and back and can lead to injuries. Unfortunately, many people can only train after dark in the winter, and are forced to run on the roads. If this is the case, it is sensible to invest in a good pair of training shoes with a thick, well-cushioned heel wedge. Many nocturnal runners also wear reflective clothing so that they are visible to drivers.

If you are very lucky, you will be able to train by running through a forest or similar terrain. This is ideal running training for orienteering as it is just what you do during a competition, so your body will get fitter in exactly the right ways. In this case it is better to train in your orienteering shoes. The ground in this type of terrain is usually so soft that there is no need to wear cushioned training shoes, and, anyway, the high heel wedges on training shoes tend to be unstable on rough ground.

## Fitness training for the young

If you are young and still growing – under the age of 16, say – the best way to train is by taking part in a variety of different sports and activities to develop all-round fitness. When the body is still growing it is dangerous to do large amounts of running, especially on roads, as the repetitive impacts can result in damage to the developing joints. Interval training is not recommended for under-17s, as there is also a risk of damaging the heart at this age. There is little point in doing a high mileage in training as the courses in the junior classes up to H17 and D17 are relatively short and there is less need for the high level of stamina required in the H21 and D21 classes. It is best to run just a couple of times a week, in addition to competing at the weekend, and then to burn up any remaining energy in other sports and activities.

## Different types of training

Training runs can be varied in a number of ways in order to make them fun. They can also be designed so that they develop specific aspects of fitness. When deciding what kind of training sessions to do, it is important to have a clear idea of what you are trying to achieve.

Never forget the obvious fact that as an orienteer you should be aiming to improve *orienteering* fitness. Orienteering involves running for 30 to 90 minutes over rough, hilly terrain. This requires stamina, strength, flexibility and agility. In addition, orienteering involves a stop/go style of running: sections of difficult navigation require you to slow down, but in between these you can run hard and fast. During the fast sections you may be running above your 'aerobic threshold'; in this state, your body cannot take in enough oxygen and as a result lactic acid (a waste product of muscle activity) builds up, causing a feeling of extreme fatigue in the muscles. The slow sections give your body a chance to recover. In fact, the physical demands of orienteering are very different to those of, say, long-distance road running, in which marathon runners aim to run at a steady pace throughout the race, somewhere just below their aerobic threshold.

In addition to requiring a rapid rate of recovery, orienteering demands more strength and agility than any other type of running. Orienteers tend to develop a bounding running style — lifting their knees and feet in order to clear rocks, branches and undergrowth. This is very different to the economical 'shuffle' of road runners, yet it is the most efficient way of negotiating forest terrain.

As well as bearing in mind the specific demands of orienteering, you should consider your own personal strengths and weaknesses when deciding what kinds of training session to use. It is better to concentrate on improving your weaknesses rather than your strengths; for example, if you are not very good at running up hills, you may decide to include hill running and hill sessions in your training.

## Types of training session:

- Going orienteering – this is the best physical training of all for orienteering, because it includes all the right ingredients in one single session!
- Running in the terrain – this involves training in forests and on heaths and moorlands, avoiding running on paths as much as possible. Terrain running is an important aspect of orienteering fitness. Training on rough ground develops strength and agility and an efficient terrain running style.
- Hill running – many orienteering areas are hilly to some extent, so if possible your training runs should include running up and down hills.
- Long runs – orienteering events require a fair degree of stamina. Long runs should be at least as long as the races that you are aiming for, and preferably 50 per cent longer, in order to improve stamina to the required level. Whenever possible, long runs should be over terrain, or at least on a soft surface, to reduce the risk of injury. Long runs should not be too slow – if you can talk comfortably all the time, you are probably not tiring yourself enough to be gaining any training benefit.
- Other forms of racing – athletics, cross-country running, fell racing and road running are all good training for orienteering. Taking part in a race often provides the motivation to run hard that is lacking in a training run.
- Pace runs – these are runs at a fastish pace for about one half to three-quarters of your normal race distance.
- Fartlek – this is a Swedish word roughly translated as 'speed-play'. It is a form of training where you run some sections hard – perhaps just the uphill parts – and other sections more easily. Hard sections can last between 30 seconds and five minutes. You can make up the session as you go along, or you may have a set routine that you follow each week. Like all types of training, it is more fun with other people.
- Interval training – interval sessions can be the hardest form of training, but they have a dramatic effect on speed, endurance and, especially relevant to orienteering, speed of recovery. Intervals involve a period of hard running followed by a period of recovery – usually slow jogging or walking around. Typical sessions might be: 20 × 200m, with 20 seconds' recovery; 10 × 400m, with 45

seconds' recovery; or 6 × 800m, with 90 seconds' recovery. Intervals of about 800m are probably the most beneficial to orienteers. To reduce the risk of injury, interval sessions should only be done after a good warm-up and preferably on a soft, even surface. They should be done at least once a week to gain the maximum benefit. Finally, remember that intervals are hard! They are not recommended for the under-17s or over-50s.

- Hill sessions – these are very like intervals in that they involve repeated bursts of running with recovery periods in between. The hard efforts take place up a hill, and the recoveries usually take the form of jogging back down. Hill sessions improve recovery in the same way that intervals do, and have the added bonus of developing leg strength. Perhaps surprisingly, many athletes find that hill sessions also improve running speed on the flat. It is easy to get injured by suddenly launching into a regime of hill sessions, so it is important to warm up well, and to start off with relatively easy sessions.

- Other sports – sports involving strength and agility will all provide excellent training for the terrain running side of orienteering fitness. They also provide variety and a break from running. Variety is a good thing in a training programme, as it reduces the risk of injury.

- Circuit training – this is a series of short exercises usually carried out indoors in a gym. Each exercise is performed for perhaps 30 seconds, followed by a 30-second rest. The exercises may include press-ups, pull-ups, sit-ups, skipping, bench-jumps, shuttle-runs and star-jumps. Circuit training is much more fun with a group of people, and many orienteering clubs organize evening sessions during the winter. It can be combined with aerobics, another excellent form of training.

- Warming up – this is not really a session in itself, but something that precedes other sessions. Your body will be more prone to injury and will not work with maximum efficiency unless it is gradually warmed up by gentle exercise. It is especially important to warm up before races or hard training sessions – 15 minutes of jogging is about right, although this figure can be reduced if it is a hot day. Many orienteering events include a jog to the start, and this provides a good opportunity for warming up.

- Stretching exercises – these are important in reducing the risk of injury and are covered on page 81.

- Rest – perhaps the most important training of all: sleeping, eating and lying on the settee are all excellent forms of rest training! Any training programme should include sufficient time to recover from hard sessions.

## Making a weekly plan

Having chosen which of the above training sessions you wish to include in your programme, the next stage is to fit them into a weekly plan. You should consider factors such as when you have time available, when there are organized training sessions with your club, and any other commitments you may have. These factors may pre-determine the shape of your weekly plan.

Many athletes follow a hard/easy plan, so that 'hard' days of training are followed by 'easy' recovery days. A weekly plan may include four hard days and three easy days, with the four hard days carefully chosen to concentrate on specific aspects of orienteering fitness. This method is more effective than a training plan in which each day is neither hard nor easy, and each run has no particular purpose. Many athletes also alternate hard and easy weeks of training.

A typical weekly plan is outlined below. The level of training described would be appropriate for an experienced orienteer in the H/D19, 21 or 35 category (see page 106), who has several years of training background.

| Day | Session | Time in minutes | Intensity |
| --- | --- | --- | --- |
| MONDAY | Recovery from Sunday's event; rest day | 0 | EASY |
| TUESDAY | Evening intervals with club, 6 × 800m | 60 | HARD |
| WEDNESDAY | Easy jog and stretching | 30 | EASY |
| THURSDAY | Afternoon off work, long run in forest | 90 | HARD |
| FRIDAY | Lots on at work | 0 | EASY |
| SATURDAY | Fartlek session with friends | 60 | HARD |
| SUNDAY | Orienteering event plus warm-up and stretching | 90 | HARD |
| | | TOTAL: 330 | |

Note how each session has a purpose and is aimed at improving one or more aspects of orienteering fitness. There is also plenty of rest. Finally, there are no 'mediocre' sessions which are neither hard nor easy, and lack any real point.

The plan shown above is only an example. Depending on your fitness and training background, your optimum level may be more or less than this. The very best orienteers in the world follow a training regime which is similar to that of other international-class athletes, and in fact many of them represent their countries at other events, such as the marathon or hill running. They frequently train twice in a day and may reach weekly totals of up to 18 hours. At the other end of the scale, a newcomer to running may aim to run just once or twice each week. In either situation, a great deal of effort can be saved if you have a positive plan and know exactly what you are trying to achieve.

## Making a year plan

This section is for the ambitious orienteer who is no longer content to train just to achieve generally better results, but is aiming to do as well as possible in a few major races each year. By drawing up a year plan, it is possible to structure running training in order to be on top form at the right time of year. Figure 10.2 shows a plan for a typical year. The process of drawing up the plan is described here.

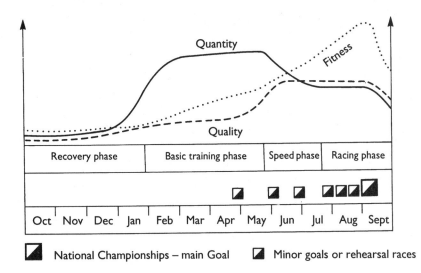

10.2 A training year plan, aiming to peak for a national championship in September.

## Choosing goals

The first step when working out a year plan is to decide upon your goals, in other words to choose those events that you particularly want to do well in. The idea of a year plan is to reach a high level of fitness, or 'peak', for a period of several weeks. This period should include your chosen goals. In figure 10.2, the main goal is an imaginary national championship in September, together with some lesser goals of regional championships in the preceding weeks.

As well as choosing a particular race as a goal, it helps to have some idea of how well you want to do in the race. You may want to finish in the first five or the first 20, or you may prefer to look at it differently and aim to finish within ten minutes of the winner. Either way, having this target in the back of your mind should help you get motivated. It is important that your goal is realistic, something you know you can achieve – it is hard to get motivated if you are aiming for the impossible!

## Training phases

Your year plan should include different phases designed to lay the foundations for the year's training and to introduce different aspects of running fitness at the right time. Having pencilled your goals on to your plan, the next stage is draw in the different phases.

---

### Training phases

---

- Basic Training Phase – this is sometimes called the 'winter training phase' because it usually takes place out of season, during the winter months. The purpose of this phase is to build up a basic level of fitness and stamina which will then last through the summer. It should last for the three or four months just before the racing season (in figure 10.2 the racing season is in the summer). Before the basic phase it is usual to spend a month or so building up your level of training so that there is no sudden increase at the start of the phase. The basic phase should then include a lot of 'quantity' – long, steady runs. Harder, faster running, or 'quality' training, is left until nearer the racing season. During the basic phase the following types of session are most appropriate: long, even-paced runs (longer than you would expect to be out for in an event); terrain runs; orienteering events (even though your target races are many months away, there is no need to stop competing); other sports; stretching and mobility sessions, and plenty of recovery.

- Speed phase – in figure 10.2, this phase coincides with the competition season during late spring and summer. As its name suggests, the aim of the speed phase is to develop running speed – after the basic phase you will be very fit in terms of strength and stamina, but will be lacking the ability to run fast. During this phase you should be doing less training than during the basic phase in terms of overall distance, but you should be running harder and faster. In other words, quantity is reduced but quality is increased. During the speed phase the following types of session are most appropriate: interval sessions; hill sessions; fartlek; generally faster runs; orienteering events, and participation in athletics, road races, cross country and hill races, if you enjoy these sports. It is still important to run in terrain as much as possible, and to continue to do a few long runs.

- Racing phase – this phase lasts for perhaps six weeks. Your major goal should be at the end of this period, and there should be other major races in the earlier part of the phase which you can use as rehearsals in which to practise racing skills before the major goal. Your main aims during the racing phase should be to 'sharpen up', in other words to carry on the speed training of the speed phase, and to get plenty of rest, so you are not tired before the races. It is important to listen to your body during this phase and not to train if you feel tired. Racing itself is very tiring, so much of this phase will be spent either resting before races or recovering afterwards. During the racing phase these sessions are most appropriate: orienteering events; rest and recovery; intervals; hill sessions; fastish runs, and other types of competitive running.

- Recovery phase – this phase should be drawn into the year plan between the end of the racing phase and beginning of next season's basic phase. The aim of the phase is to let your body recover from the exertions of the other phases. It is unwise to train hard all year round without some kind of rest period. During the recovery phase it is a good idea to keep ticking over by going running, but your weekly totals should be only about 50 or 65 per cent of what they are during the basic phase. The recovery phase is a good chance to take part in some other sports: mountain biking, swimming, football, fishing, gardening, watching television! If you picked up any recurring minor injuries during the competition season, then the recovery phase provides an opportunity to get them sorted out.

## *Allowing for injury or illness*

You should never train if you feel at all ill, and if you are injured it is often necessary to rest for a few days or weeks (see the later sections in this chapter). When you draw up your year plan, you should allow for periods of time when you cannot run. For example: if you wish to train hard for 16 weeks during the basic phase, you should add an extra two weeks to the length of the phase in case you pick up a cold or minor injury. Taking time off to recover from illness or injury can be very frustrating, but it is much easier to cope with psychologically if it is already built into your plan.

## *Planning for two peaks*

The year plan can be adapted to enable you to peak twice during one season. For example: in the British season the major domestic races are held in the spring, and this period would represent the first racing phase. The second racing phase would then follow a couple of months later; in Britain this would include the big 'holiday events', such as the Scottish Six-Days, which take place towards the end of summer. Other countries stage similar multi-day events at this time of year, and many orienteers choose to travel abroad to race at this time. In order to peak twice, it is necessary to go through the basic and speed phases before the first racing phase, then to repeat this process before the second racing phase. As there is not much time between the two racing phases, the basic and speed phases will have to be condensed the second time round. For example: you may return to basic training for just four weeks, and then to speed training for just two weeks, before the second racing phase. Some athletes attempt to peak three or more times during a season, but the resulting training plan is so complex that it is difficult to put into practice.

# Keeping a training diary

It is useful to keep a record of your past training. You may feel the need to look back at the training you have done over the last few years or months in order to work out what went wrong: why you became injured, for example. On the other hand, your training may have gone very well, and you may wish to look at what training you did so that you can repeat it in the future.

A training diary enables you to keep track of the amount of training you have done. This is important, because it is not a good idea to increase the amount you do by more than about 10 per cent each year.

Writing down your training in a diary can also provide valuable motivation – you can see whether you are reaching you training targets. However, it can be dangerous to chase targets too religiously, for instance by trying to reach a certain mileage each week, as this can lead you to ignore the warning signs that your body is tired and in need of a rest.

It is possible to buy special orienteering training diaries from mobile shops at events.

## Illness and training

The golden rule is never to train if you feel at all ill. It is extremely dangerous to engage in strenuous exercise if you have a viral or bacterial infection, however slight it may seem, as certain types of infection can spread to the heart muscle, and may even result in death. Several top orienteers have tragically died in recent years for this reason. In any case, recovery from a cold or other infection is considerably delayed by continuing to train; it is better to stop running completely until the illness has cleared up, which should only take a few days. Although it is frustrating to miss what at the time seems vital training, in the long term the loss of a few days makes no difference at all to your fitness.

Many athletes record their pulse on waking up in the morning. If your pulse is raised by a significant amount – say ten to 15 beats per minute above its normal resting rate – this is a sign that you could be going down with an illness. It is also very often a sign of tiredness, resulting from overtraining. In either case, the best thing to do is to stop running for a day or two to give your resting pulse a chance to return to normal.

Athletes who are training hard are particularly susceptible to minor infections such as colds and 'flu. To reduce the risk of getting ill, avoid overtraining and keep warm after exercise. You should also take care with your diet and drink sufficient fluids, such as electrolyte sports drinks, especially in hot weather.

## Injuries

Sports injuries and their treatment is a vast and specialized subject. This section deals with the basics of how to avoid getting injured, and gives some simple advice on what to do when you do. If your injury is at all severe, or you have any doubts, seek professional medical advice.

## Avoiding injuries

Orienteering injuries fall into two categories. The first are 'overuse injuries', which are caused by many repeated stresses and impacts to one particular part of the body, perhaps as a result of a lot of running on hard surfaces. The second type are 'traumatic injuries', which are caused by a single accident. Included in this category are sprains, cuts, bruises and fractures.

---

### Guidelines for avoiding overuse injuries:

---

- Avoid running on roads and hard surfaces as much as possible. Try to train in terrain whenever you can. A soft, uneven surface is much easier on the legs.
- Wear good shoes with plenty of heel cushioning if you have to train on the roads. Do not wear old, worn-out shoes. However, bear in mind that new shoes may cause aches and pains while you are getting used to them, and that it is not a good idea to do a long run in a brand-new pair.
- Check the soles of your shoes to see if they are wearing and compacting more on the inside than on the outside, or vice versa. If your foot is tilting inwards (pronation) or outwards (supination) on impact with the ground, you could be placing a lot of strain on various parts of your legs. Both conditions can be rectified with expert advice.
- Never suddenly increase the amount of training that you do, or try to come back too quickly after an injury. Equally, never suddenly change the type of training that you do.
- Warm up before a race or hard session, and do plenty of regular stretching exercises.

---

Traumatic injuries are to some extent an unavoidable result of running through terrain; everyone falls over now and then and sustains cuts and bruises when they are racing hard. Despite this, the seriousness of many of these injuries can be reduced by warming up well. It also helps if you are used to running in terrain and are strong, agile, and flexible as a result of stretching exercises. It is important not to wear loose or poorly fitting shoes, as these can make it difficult to balance on rough ground, cause blisters and sprained ankles.

**10.3** Stretching exercises to improve mobility and flexibility, and reduce the risk of injury. Warm up first, and then for each exercise gradually stretch into position, holding for about 20 seconds before relaxing.

## Stretching

Stretching exercises are vital to keep your muscles and joints flexible and mobile, thereby reducing the risk of injury. An unfortunate side effect of running is that it tends to reduce flexibility and to shorten the muscle fibres, so stretching exercises should be used to reverse this process as part of a training programme.

81

Stretching should be done at least a couple of times each week. Figure 10.3 illustrates a number of different exercises, designed to stretch different muscle groups. Warm up by jogging before you start. When stretching, it is very important not to make any jerky movements. It is common to see athletes on television who jerk and bounce when they stretch: they might be highly paid, but they do not know how to stretch properly! Gradually stretch into a position, then stop when it would be painful or uncomfortable to go any further. Hold this position for about 20 seconds, then relax and move on to the next exercise. Repeat the whole session two or three times, aiming to achieve an increased range of movement each time.

## Treating injuries

If you have just sustained an injury, you can treat yourself immediately and effectively by following the **RICE** formula.

**R** stands for Rest: stop running to give the injury a chance to recover. Avoid loading the injured part.

**I** stands for Ice: place an ice pack or a bag filled with ice cubes on the injured part for 15 minutes. Do not put ice directly on to your skin – cover it with a piece of cloth or a towel first. If you are out in the terrain and cannot get hold of any ice, then you may be able to immerse the injury in a stream. The cooling effect of ice reduces swelling and inflammation in the damaged tissues, and speeds recovery.

**C** stands for Compression. Applying pressure to the injured part, perhaps with a compression bandage, is another way of reducing inflammation.

**E** stands for Elevation. Keeping the injury raised also reduces inflammation.

It is possible to buy effective anti-inflammatory drugs over the counter, such as ibuprofen, but beware – these can cause stomach upsets. They also have the effect of masking pain, and can mislead you into running on an injury before it has healed sufficiently. Some other drugs are banned in sport under international doping rules. You will be able to obtain a list of banned medications from your national orienteering federation.

If you have sustained an overuse injury, you should think carefully about the possible causes. Perhaps there is something wrong with your shoes and you should consider replacing them. Look back through your training diary: the cause is often something quite obvious, like a sudden increase in training, more road running or a particularly hard hill session. You may be able to cure the injury simply by a change in your training.

Many athletes try to 'train through' injuries in the hope that they will recover without resting and thereby will not miss any training. Sometimes this is possible, but many injuries have a habit of starting out as slight aches or niggles and then getting worse and worse if they are neglected. It is always worthwhile treating the injury, seeking expert advice if necessary, resting until it gets better, and trying to find out what caused it.

## Seeking advice

The best people to turn to if you need advice about an injury are doctors or qualified physiotherapists who specialize in sports injuries. They can often be visited at sports injury clinics and will be familiar with the urgency felt by athletes following a training programme, so their priority will be to get you back running as soon as possible. As well as providing a diagnosis and treatment, they should be able to give you rehabilitation exercises to help cure the injury and strengthen that part of the body, so that the injury will not recur in the future.

## Two common orienteering injuries

**Sprained ankles** are the most common and one of the most frustrating of injuries suffered by orienteers. A single slip or misplaced step whilst running in rough terrain can result in a sudden, painful wrench of the ankle followed by a swelling and soreness that may last for several weeks. Even after this time, the ankle can remain in a weakened state for months. The first thing to do after spraining an ankle is to follow the RICE formula (see page 82). If there is no ice around, put your foot in a stream. If the sprain is severe, then seek medical advice. The ankle may need to be X-rayed to check that it is not broken.

Try to avoid putting weight on the ankle for the first few days if it is very swollen and sore, but as soon after the injury as possible exercise the ankle by moving your foot in an up-and-down motion with no load on it. Start walking when you are able to do so without feeling pain, and then start running short distances on a level surface. Take great care not to sprain the ankle again, as it will still be very weak and the reflex nerves that stop it from going over may be damaged. Ankle taping is a way of strapping up a weak ankle before each run so that it is less likely to go over again. One method of ankle taping is shown in figure 10.4. Use rigid (non-stretchy) zinc oxide tape with a width of

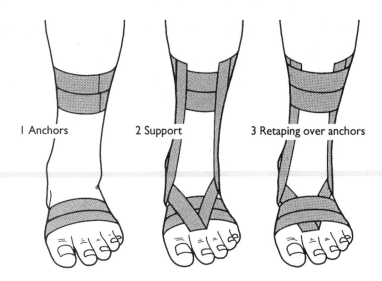

| I Anchors | 2 Support | 3 Retaping over anchors |

**10.4** Three stages in ankle taping.

about 4cm (1½in). It is possible to buy a spray that helps the tape stick to skin. It is important that the tape does not restrict your normal running action, otherwise it will quickly tear or pull off. Take care also to prevent the tape from rubbing on your Achilles or any other tendon. The tape should prevent your ankle from going right over, but failing this it should at least slow down the rolling action of a potential sprain and give a warning tug on your skin, so that you have time to stop the ankle from going over fully.

Sprained ankles can be strengthened simply by balancing on one foot. This retrains your coordination and strengthens the muscles and nerves. As your ankle improves you can progress to a wobble-board. This is a flat board mounted on a hemisphere, the idea being to try to balance on the board. You should start exercising as soon as possible after the injury, provided that you can do so without pain. After a severe sprain you may need to keep up the exercises for up to six months. A qualified physiotherapist will be able to give specialist treatment and advice on strengthening exercises.

**Blisters** can be painful enough to reduce the toughest competitor to a hobble! They are caused by friction on the feet, perhaps as a result of shoes which are either too loose or too tight, of running across steep slopes, or of running on hard ground in hot conditions.

If you are out training, you may become aware that your feet are getting sore before blisters actually develop. In this situation it is well worth stopping to fiddle around with your shoes and socks. You could try removing the insole from your shoe. During a race, however, you may be unable to stop, but before your next run you may be able to do something to your shoes to prevent the blisters from being further aggravated, perhaps by inserting extra insoles, wearing a different type of sock or two pairs of thin socks, cutting holes in the shoes, or even throwing them away and getting a new pair! You can protect the blisters themselves with self-adhesive chiropody felt: a hole is cut in the felt which is placed over the blister to keep it free from any pressure. Another effective treatment is to use a 'second-skin' material. This is a specially manufactured layer of gooey plastic that is placed over the blister to act as an extra layer of skin. Alternatively, the application of a lubricant such as vaseline may help to prevent the blister from chafing.

To prevent blisters occurring, you should use a pumice stone to remove hard skin from under the foot, especially under the big toe. Areas that are liable to blister can be covered with a proprietary protective covering before each run.

If you need to burst a blister in order to run comfortably, you should take care to prevent it from becoming infected. Make a small hole in the bottom of the blister with a sterile needle, then cover the area with antiseptic cream and apply a dressing.

## First aid

First aid is a large subject and is really beyond the scope of this book; the *Outward Bound First Aid Handbook* deals in depth with first aid in an outdoor situation. Many charitable first aid organizations run short instructional courses and these are highly recommended for anyone, not just sportspeople. In a few hours it is possible to learn how to save lives by resuscitation, as well as how to treat less serious injuries.

---

### First aid kit

---

The following items should be included in an orienteering first aid kit:

- Sterile dressings
- Plasters
- Crêpe bandages
- Antiseptic wipes
- Scissors
- Sterile needles
- Tweezers

- Safety pins
- Padding for blisters
- Antiseptic cream
- Chemical ice packs
- Cream for stings
- Permissible painkillers/anti-inflammatories

---

# 11

# Orienteering technique training

This chapter describes a number of exercises that you can use to improve your map-reading and compass skills. Many orienteers just take part in competitions and never bother with technique training, and as a result they rarely get a chance to think about what they are doing wrong, or to learn new skills or improve existing skills. During a race it is tempting just to rush along using the same old bad habits.

Some time and effort is required to travel out to a suitable area in order to practise techniques. The exercises here are all more fun if you do them with a group of people, and you can then put out markers for each other. Technique training can be very enjoyable: it is a relaxing experience to orienteer with the whole course to yourself, and very different to the pressure and bustle of a competition.

Each exercise described in this chapter is aimed at one specific technique. Before you start technique training you should try to work out exaxctly where your strengths and weaknesses lie, and then choose exercises aimed at improving the weaknesses. You should be critical of your mistakes in races and training, and then try to analyse them in order to find out what went wrong and how your technique could be improved. Before doing any technique training you should also consider the type of terrain available to you, as it may not be suitable for certain kinds of exercise.

Technique training is most relevant just before and during the competition season, and can be built into a year plan such as the one described in the previous chapter. During each exercise you should concentrate hard on the technique that you are aiming to improve. Keep each exercise short – say 15 to 30 minutes – so that you are able to concentrate fully throughout. Always make sure to get things right. Start off slowly, and slow down if you are making mistakes. Persevere with new techniques; they may seem awkward at first, but it will be worthwhile in the long run.

# Technique training exercises

## Accurate compass and distance estimation

In this exercise, all the detail is removed from the map apart from the control circles. Each leg is fairly short, between 100m and 300m, and the fine-orienteering skills of accurate compass and distance estimation or pace counting are used to find the markers (figure 11.1a). This exercise is more realistic in relatively flat, featureless terrain.

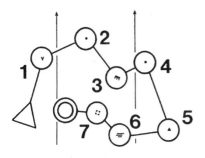

**11.1a** Compass and distance estimation: apart from the control features, all the detail has been removed from the map.

## Control picking

This exercise consists of a series of short legs in detailed terrain, the aim being to practise finding controls using fine map-reading (visualization and continuous contact) and fine compass (figure 11.1b). In effect, each control is the attack point for the next one. A few long, easy legs can be included to provide a mental rest.

**11.1b** A series of short legs in detailed terrain, demanding concentration and continuous fine orienteering skills.

## Line orienteering

In this exercise, you try to follow a wiggly line drawn through a detailed part of the map (figure 11.1c). Keep the map constantly set with the compass. This is a fine-orienteering exercise and is excellent training for continuous-contact map-reading. It requires intense concentration, so should not be longer than 1.5–2km.

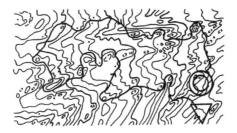

**II.Ic** An exercise in which the aim is to follow the line as closely as possible – excellent training for continuous-contact orienteering.

## *Slope orienteering*

This is control picking but on a steep slope and is a fine-orienteering exercise (figure 11.1d). Try to set the legs at a variety of angles across the slope and think about the special problems of orienteering on a slope. For example: does the slope pull you downhill when you are contouring? How can you use relative heights and the angle of the slope as an aid to navigation?

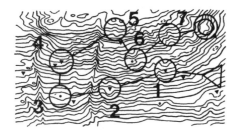

**II.Id** Fine orienteering on a slope: a series of short legs set at a variety of angles to the slope.

## *Rough orienteering I*

This exercise consists of a series of medium or longish legs – 600–1000m each – with the controls hung visibly on large features (figure 11.2a). The idea is to use rough compass and map simplification to get to the control as quickly as possible.

## *Rough orienteering II*

A variation on the previous exercise, here the map is blanked out for the middle section of the leg (figure 11.2b). The idea is to cross the blanked-out section quickly and accurately on rough compass. This exercise also trains mid-leg relocation as, having crossed the blanked-out section, it is necessary to relocate.

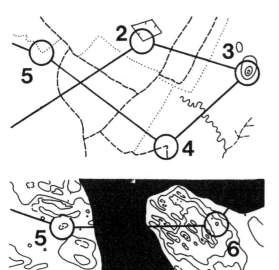

**11.2a** Long legs have been planned between obvious control sites, with the aim of crossing the terrain quickly and accurately using rough-orienteering skills.

**11.2b** Sections of the map have been blacked out in order to place a premium on accurate rough compass.

## Relocation near the control

Each leg of this exercise is about 500m long. Run as a pair, with one map: the leader orienteers to a point within 200m of the control and then hands over the map to the other runner, who has to relocate and find the control (figure 11.3a).

## Relocation in mid-leg

This time, each leg is 500–800m long and should be set so that the best route is roughly a straight line (figure 11.3b). Run as a pair, with one map. The leader runs hard to a point in the middle of the leg and then hands over the map to the other runner, who has to keep running, relocate on the move and continue to the control. When following, it helps to try to remember the features that you pass and to keep checking the compass to see what direction the leader is taking.

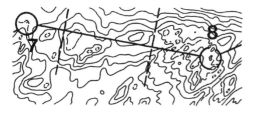

**11.3a** Relocation in mid-leg: an exercise for pairs of runners using one map. The leader hands over the map somewhere between the two dashed lines to his partner, who then has to continue to the control without slowing down.

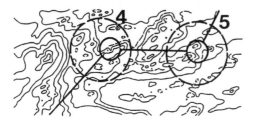

**11.3 b** Relocation near the control: another pairs exercise. This time, the map is handed over anywhere within the larger circle.

## Route choice

Plan a course with medium to long legs which each have several alternative routes (figure 11.4). Run as a group of two or more. Before starting, decide who will run each route; then start off together on each leg and see who gets to the control first, or time each route. Many orienteers wear 'split watches' with a stopwatch function that can record up to 30 split times. These can then be compared after training sessions and races.

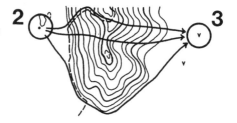

**11.4** Route-choice exercise for two or more runners. Each takes a different route and the times taken are then compared.

## Contour-only training

This excellent form of training can transform a mediocre orienteering area into a formidable, technically challenging piece of terrain. Only the contours are shown on the map, which may be a photocopy of the brown tracing from the original map artwork – all the line features such as paths, fences and streams are absent. Contour-only maps can be used for all the exercises described here, as well as being ideal for learning about contours.

## Map-making

Have a go at mapping a small, detailed section of terrain – many forests have small areas of old quarries or diggings which are ideal for this exercise. Concentrate on drawing the contour shapes. This gives an understanding of the way maps are made and provides an insight into the problems facing map-makers.

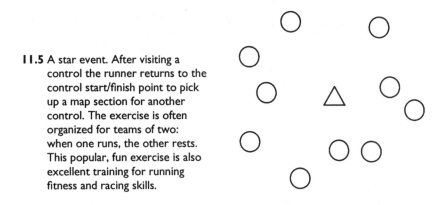

**11.5** A star event. After visiting a control the runner returns to the control start/finish point to pick up a map section for another control. The exercise is often organized for teams of two: when one runs, the other rests. This popular, fun exercise is also excellent training for running fitness and racing skills.

## Control flow

Set an easy course with short legs. Concentrate on the routine of planning ahead, looking at the next leg, remembering codes, punching quickly and generally running through the controls smoothly. Do not worry too much about getting the actual navigation right.

# Fun exercises

These are exercises for a group of people, where the aim is enjoyment as well as technique training. They are useful as part of the programme for a training camp, as they provide relief from other more intense exercises. An element of competition is often introduced to make these exercises more exciting. With some imagination, the exercises described here can be varied endlessly.

## Mini-relays

Each team has two or three runners. The first-loop runners start together in a mass start and then complete a course, usually only 2–3km, before handing over to the second-loop runners, and so on. The first team back is the winner.

## Star events

Everyone starts from a central point. The controls are arranged in a circle about 200–400m from this point (figure 11.5). Each runner gets a section of map showing just one control. From the mass start they visit this control, then return to the start to get a map section for another control, and so on until someone has visited all the controls. This exercise can be organized as a relay for teams of two.

### Trains

This exercise consists of several short loops or sections of 1.5–2km. Runners are started at intervals of about 15 or 20 seconds, with the slowest starting first. The runners tend to bunch together into groups, or 'trains', and the resulting fast, competitive orienteering is excellent practice for relay running.

### The Palmer challenge

This was devised by Peter Palmer, an inspirational coach who has done much to lay the foundations of coaching in Great Britain. The two members of an equally matched pair run against each other. They are each given a map showing a control site. They run to this site and hang a marker there, then continue to their opponent's control site, where they collect their opponent's marker. The first one back wins.

## Indoor exercises

During the winter months it can be difficult to get to suitable terrain technique training. An alternative is to do indoor exercises, which can be included as part of a gym session such as circuit training, or can even be done in the civilized setting of a comfortable armchair.

Indoor exercises may involve solving route-choice problems on map sections, for instance during the recovery periods between shuttle runs in a gym. Or you may be given 30 seconds to memorize a leg on the map, then a further 30 seconds to draw the main features on a sheet of paper (difficult!). A good exercise is to try to describe, in words but without referring to bearings or distances, the positions of control sites on a map to someone who has a blank copy of the same map.

Orienteering magazines sometimes run photo-orienteering competitions. The idea is to plot the positions of control sites on to a blank map using a single photo of each site, together with the direction from which the photo was taken. There are also a few crude computer games that mimic orienteering. With powerful computers now readily available, it is only a matter of time before more sophisticated games are developed.

## Self-analysis

After each event, it is a good idea to draw your route on the map. Think about the possible causes of any mistakes that you may have made. Were they compass mistakes, or were they caused by poor map interpretation? How can you avoid making similar mistakes in the future? Even if your routes look perfect and you did not make any mistakes, there may still be ways in which you can get faster. Were you being over-cautious on the easy parts of the course?

Some orienteers tend to be slightly complacent about their abilities as navigators. On the whole, orienteers resent being told that they are bad map-readers in the same way that motorists hate being told that they are bad drivers! However the very best orienteers are constantly self-critical and are always watchful for flaws in their technique.

It is easy to attribute one or two bad mistakes to a 'sudden lack of concentration', especially if the other controls on the course posed no problems, but very often the real cause is inadequate technique. It is often possible to find 90 per cent of the controls with no problems, even orienteering poorly: it is the other 10 per cent that are significant and indicate a flawed technique. In any case, a very good orienteer will have the technical ability to find controls even when their concentration is failing.

## Coaching orienteering

Coaching can be a rewarding and enjoyable activity. Many coaches prefer instructing orienteering to actually competing, but coaching is not an easy way out for failed orienteers! A coach always has to be one step ahead of the athletes, and needs a good knowledge of the technical and physical aspects of the sport – coaches often find that their own orienteering improves as a result of teaching others. Coaching can take place on many different levels, from teaching or instructing groups of young beginners, perhaps in a school or outdoor centre, through to looking after a group of elite orienteers such as a national team on a tour abroad.

A coach should be a source of ideas. Experienced orienteers may pick and choose from these, accepting those ideas that they feel are relevant to themselves and rejecting the others. Ultimately, however, the best coach an athlete can have is themselves, as they are able to monitor their own mind and body better than anyone else. So, as the relationship between a coach and an athlete progresses, the coach should gradually have less and less input and the athlete should become more and more independent.

### Setting training exercises

This is a fundamental part of the coach's job. Depending on the technique to be worked on, the coach may choose between any of the different exercises described in the previous section, or may devise a completely new exercise.

The length and difficulty of each exercise has to be carefully matched to the athlete's ability. Most people find it difficult to concentrate hard for more than 20 or 30 minutes at a time, so training exercises should not be too long. A good idea is to plan a series of mini-exercises in the form of short loops, with the runners returning to a central point for a rest after each loop.

The type of exercise set has to be appropriate to the terrain available and to the limitations of the map. Each exercise should be introduced with a clear briefing to explain its purpose. Above all, a coach should bear in mind that technique training must be enjoyable in order to be effective.

## Shadowing

Orienteering is one of the hardest sports to coach. It is often impossible to watch people orienteering, as they are hidden in the depths of the terrain for most of the time, so it is hard to see where they going wrong. In addition, orienteering techniques largely take place in the head of the runner, and it is difficult to know what people are thinking without being a mind-reader.

Shadowing involves following a runner through the course in order to observe them orienteering, and is a very demanding part of coaching. Firstly, it is necessary to be as fit as the person you are following. In addition, you have to be constantly aware of your position on the map, even if your pupil has no idea themselves. On top of this, you have to try to be aware of the techniques they are using, how well they are using them and how they could improve. For example: are they looking at the map and compass enough, are they running too fast, are they taking the wrong information from the map?

A problem with shadowing is that orienteers tend to change their style when they know they are being followed. Some become flustered and make uncharacteristic mistakes, whereas others concentrate harder than they would normally do and make no mistakes at all. A way of getting round this is to run alternate legs – the coach and pupil take turns to lead. The pupil then feels part of a team with the coach and forgets that he or she is being scrutinized.

The coach should only stop the runner to give advice at the controls, rather than interrupting the flow in mid-leg. The coach may discuss what went wrong on the last leg, and talk through the route on the next leg. Any advice given should be succinct and to the point – it is difficult to think about more than one new technique at a time.

## Teaching orienteering to the young

Orienteering is being taught more and more in schools and outdoor centres, and can provide a link between many subjects in a school curriculum. As well as being good physical exercise, it includes elements of mathematics, geography and art, especially if map-making is included. In outdoor education, orienteering is less dangerous than many other activities such as climbing, canoeing or abseiling. As a result, students do not need such close supervision; they are more independent and can make decisions for themselves. Orienteering also has a competitive element which is lacking from most other outdoor activities. All teachers of orienteering should have been to at least one event themselves, as this will help them convey the special excitement of the sport to their pupils.

The first two things to teach a group of beginners of any age are the idea that the map is a picture of the ground, and how to set the map with the ground features. It is a good idea to take the group on a short 'map walk' in order to introduce these concepts, and to explain the different map symbols and get a feel for the map scale. Point out features as you walk along, and make sure that everyone has the map set. The idea of the map as a picture can also be introduced using a map of a classroom or playground. Beginners should be encouraged to orienteer by map-reading; fitting the map to the ground and following the features. The compass can be introduced at a later stage.

When planning exercises, the main priority is that everyone should get around successfully and finish with a smile. Each exercise should be very short. The courses and control sites should be totally fair: beginners are easily thrown by poor maps. Above all, the controls should be hung visibly and in the right place. The following are two examples of teaching progressions for orienteering.

---

### A map progression:

---

- Session 1 – a classroom map at 1:50 is used to introduce map scales, the map as a picture and setting the map. The students can map the classroom themselves and set out courses.
- Session 2 – a playground/grounds map at about 1:1000 is used for short, fun exercises such as star relays.

- Session 3 – a local park map at about 1:5000 is used for this session. There may be a permanent course which can be used as the basis for fun exercises and competitions.
- Session 4 – into the forest! This session uses a local area of simple terrain with plenty of line features, mapped at 1:10 000, and ideally with a permanent course. This could be a simple score event – 30 minutes to visit as many markers as possible.

---

## A progression through exercise types:

This is useful if there is only one map available.

- Session 1 – a map walk.
- Session 2 – a cross-country type course, 1.5km with controls on easy line features.
- Session 3 – a score event.
- Session 4 – a star relay race.
- Session 5 – a cross-country type event, built up to be 'the big race' with plenty of small prizes. 2.5km with easy controls just off line features.

---

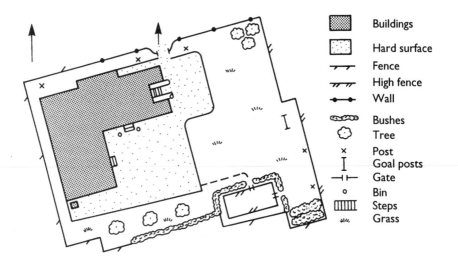

| | |
|---|---|
| ▨ | Buildings |
| ▨ | Hard surface |
| ┰┰ | Fence |
| ┰┰┰ | High fence |
| ●–●–● | Wall |
| ⬭⬭⬭ | Bushes |
| ♧ | Tree |
| × | Post |
| I | Goal posts |
| ⊢⊢ | Gate |
| o | Bin |
| ⅢⅢ | Steps |
| ⩊ | Grass |

**11.6** A playground map at a scale of 1:1000.

96

# 12

# Different types of orienteering

## Cross-country type events

Most orienteering events, including the major championships, follow the cross-country format. The control circles are numbered on the map and linked with lines, and must be visited in the order given. Competitors are started at intervals of between one and four minutes.

## Score events

In a score event, the controls can be visited in any order and each control has a points value. Competitors have a time limit, usually between 60 and 90 minutes, in which to visit as many controls as possible. There are heavy penalties for getting back late, so it is always worth finishing within the time limit. Score events are excellent for beginners or mixed-ability groups, as everyone can score at least a few points and it is not possible to be disqualified by being unable to find a control, as is the case in cross-country type events.

Before setting off from the start in a score event it is essential to spend a minute or two working out which controls to visit and in what order. It helps if you know roughly how far you can cover in the time allowed on that sort of terrain. For the first 80 per cent or so of the time allowance you should stick to a predetermined plan and concentrate on the navigation. For the remainder of the time allowance you should leave yourself several options from which to choose, depending on the exact amount of time left. It helps if there is a cluster of controls around the finish: if you leave these to last, you can then get as many of them as you can.

## Relays

Relays are an exciting and popular form of orienteering, open to teams of three or more runners. The first-loop runners start together in a mass start. At the end of their loop they hand over to the second-loop runners, and so on. The first team to finish are the winners. Each loop in a relay is only about 50–75 per cent as long as an individual race. To reduce following, relays are planned using a 'forking' system, which means that teams run their loops in different orders. In addition, each loop is made up of different sections which can be run in various combinations. At the end of the race each team will have run the same legs, although in different orders.

In a relay event, any team that produces steady runs from each of its runners will finish in a good position. Many orienteers specialize in a particular loop. First-loop runners enjoy the pressure of mass starts and respond well to having other runners around them out on the course. Second-loop runners need to be adaptable; they may be running with other people, or they may be alone. Final-loop runners are often required to make a fast finish over the last few controls in order to break away from other runners – the last loop is the only part of a relay where it is worth taking risks.

Most relays have three or four loops, but one or two notable events in the international calendar are organized on a much larger scale. The annual Tiomila in Sweden is a ten-leg relay that starts at midnight. The first loops therefore involve night orienteering, and the race does not finish until early the next morning. The similar Jukola race in Finland attracts an entry of over 1000 seven-member teams.

## Short-distance orienteering

This form of orienteering has developed fairly recently, short races being introduced as an international category at the 1991 World Championships in Czechoslovakia.

Short races are usually of between 20 and 30 minutes' duration. They are a supreme test of speed control and technique: it is possible to run very fast over such short distances, but danger lies in running too fast at the wrong time and making mistakes. The results are so close that it is tempting to try too hard in order to save seconds, yet at the same time a mistake of only one minute can be disastrous. Good short-distance orienteers are able to orienteer smoothly while close to their technical limits.

## Long-distance orienteering

Long-distance races (or Long-Os) can be anything up to twice as long as normal courses: often, several maps of adjoining areas are linked together. The legs between controls tend to be longer than in normal orienteering and usually include plenty of route choice.

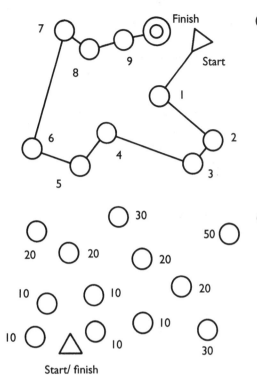

(a) The controls are numbered and joined by lines, and must be visited in the order given

(b) Each competitor visits as many controls as possible within a given time limit, in any order they like. Each control has a points value; there is a penalty for exceeding the time limit

**12.1** The two most common forms of orienteering event; (a) cross-country type, and (b) score orienteering.

# Night orienteering

Night events are organized in exactly the same way as other events, with the same maps and control markers. Not surprisingly, orienteering at night can be very tricky, and it is often worth taking long path routes that you would not consider in a daytime event. Keen night orienteers use halogen head torches powered by rechargeable battery packs.

# Mountain orienteering

This is a form of long-distance orienteering that takes place on open mountains, fells and moorland. There are few controls, long legs and route choice plays a key role. The map scales most commonly used are 1:25 000, 1:40 000 or 1:50 000. A very popular format is followed by 'mountain marathon' events. These are open to teams of two who compete over two days and carry lightweight camping gear. On the first day they run a long course that ends at a remote mid-way campsite where they are timed in. On the second day they run another course that finishes back at the event centre. The two times are added together to find the winners. Winning times may vary from three to ten hours each day. Mountain marathons are held regularly in Norway, Switzerland, Great Britain, New Zealand and Australia.

## Mountain-bike orienteering
This form of orienteering is becoming increasingly popular in different European countries. It is the youngest branch of the sport and as yet there are no set standards for course lengths, map scales and race formats. In Great Britain there are now several mountain marathon events organized for mountain bikers. A problem facing this branch of the sport is that it is not easy to find venues with a suitably complex network of tracks, bridleways and small roads where riders have a right of access.

## Ski-orienteering
This activity is widespread in Scandinavia and has its own biennial world championships. Competitors use cross-country skis and follow prepared trails which are overprinted as green lines on the map. The navigation involves a great deal of route choice, although there is no fine orienteering. The map is carried on a rotatable board which is fixed to the skier's chest, so that both hands are free to manage the ski poles. The best ski-orienteers are extremely fit skiers with a good enough skiing technique to handle poor or varied snow conditions.

## Trail orienteering
Trail orienteering is organized for disabled competitors in wheelchairs. In one form of Trail-O, the competitors are untimed and make their way between control sites that are visible from level, well-surfaced tracks. Several markers are hung at each site, but only one is in exactly the right place. Competitors score points on their ability to decide which is the correct marker. In other forms of Trail-O, the competitors are timed around cross-country type courses on well-surfaced tracks.

## Other types of orienteering
'Street events' are held on street maps of urban areas, often during winter evenings as a means of training. 'Wayfaring' is a term sometimes used to describe non-competitive, untimed orienteering which usually

takes place on a permanent course. A variety of novelty events are also occasionally organized, such as canoe orienteering, sailing orienteering or cave orienteering.

## Terrain types

Much of the appeal of orienteering lies in the variety of the terrain and scenery encountered at different events. Different kinds of terrain pose different technical problems, and experienced competitors gradually learn how to cope with the various terrain types and can often predict what the terrain will be like at a certain event. Some of the more common types of terrain are described below.

### *Continental terrain*

This term refers to a terrain type that is widespread over southern England and Central Europe (figure 12.2A). Continental terrain typically has a dense network of paths. The ground shapes are smooth and lack intricate contour detail, although the terrain can be very hilly. Control sites are typically provided by point-features such as pits, rootmounds (or rootstocks – the upturned roots of fallen trees), small knolls, or by minor line features such as ditches and vegetation changes. Rough orienteering is fairly straightforward due to the network of tracks, but finding the controls can be tricky as they are often sited on small features in otherwise featureless terrain. It is best to adopt a two-paced approach: fast running, often on paths, between the controls, and then carefully into the control circle. Route choice can be important, especially in the more hilly areas.

### *Nordic terrain*

This type of terrain is found in areas which were once eroded by glaciers. It is typical of Norway, Sweden, Finland, Russia, New England and Canada, and is also found in the Lake District and Scotland in Great Britain (figure 12.2B). The ground shapes are extremely broken and intricate and there are many marshes, boulders and crags. This terrain is very demanding, especially for the beginner, as there are few handrail features. The techniques of contour-reading and compass have to be used well. There is generally a lot of undergrowth, and numerous small ups and downs demanding strength and agility from the runner. Straight-line routes are often the best, and the orienteering tends to be more one-paced than in continental terrain.

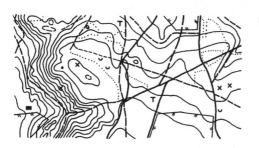

(a) Continental terrain in Germany, with a dense net-work of paths, numerous small point features and smooth, simple contour shapes

(b) Part of a map from southern Norway, depicting typical Nordic terrain with intricate, broken topography and many crags and marshes

(c) Moraine terrain in Speyside, in the Scottish Highlands. It is easy to confuse hills with depressions: the depressions are all drawn with tags point-ing inwards, whereas the knolls have no tags at all

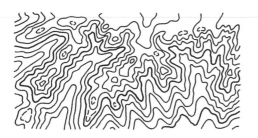

(d) Typical sand-dune ridges and hollows near Bordeaux in France. The linear fire breaks are common features of planted sand dunes

(e) Spur/gully terrain from an Australian map. The numerous parallel features can easily be confused

**12.2** Terrain types for orienteering.

## Moraine terrain

Moraine terrain is often associated with Nordic terrain. Moraines are irregular mounds and hollows formed from the pebbly or sandy material deposited by glaciers and rivers during an ice age. A feature of moraines is 'negative relief': that is, there are lots of 'down' features such as depressions and hollows, shown with closed contour rings on the map (figure 12.2C). These can be confused with the knolls and ridges. Take care when deciding what is up or down.

## Sand-dune terrain

Sand-dune areas are usually coastal. Especially fine areas are found near Bordeaux in France and on the North Island of New Zealand. The contour detail is always complex and includes many negative features, so good contour-reading is essential (figure 12.2D). Sometimes there are large parallel ridges separated by flat areas, which serve as handrails and simplify the navigation. Many dunes are planted with conifers, providing pleasant running on a carpet of pine needles. The plantations usually feature a grid system of fire breaks, which helps to simplify the rough orienteering.

## Spur/gully terrain

This is a variety of continental terrain that features numerous parallel re-entrants and spurs, the re-entrants rarely contain water features (figure 12.2E). Examples are found at Cannock Chase in England, in Jutland in Denmark, and in many parts of Australia. Route choice is important in spur/gully terrain: it can be very energy-sapping to run across the grain of the ridges. Care has to be taken not to get into the wrong re-entrant or system of re-entrants. In addition, some re-entrants divide half-way up, which can make things confusing if you are on the wrong level.

## Open terrain

Treeless terrain is commonly used for orienteering, examples being moorland areas in the British Isles and open farmland in New Zealand. Open terrain often has fewer line features than wooded terrain, and so it can seem harder at first. However, it is possible to see a lot further, which makes things easy for experienced orienteers who are good at reading contours. Very often it is possible to recognize a feature in the distance, perhaps as much as a kilometre away, which you know you have to run to, so there is no need to waste time by reading the map on the way there.

# Useful addresses

The following National Offices are able to provide information about local clubs and fixtures.

**International Orienteering Federation (IOF)**
PO Box 76
S 191 21 Sollentuna
Sweden
Fax: 46 8 35 71 68

**Australia**
Orienteering Federation of Australia
PO Box 740
Glebe NSW 2037
Tel: 61 2 660 2067
Fax: 61 2 660 6661

**Canada**
Canadian Orienteering Federation
1600 James Naismith Drive
Gloucester
Ontario K1B 5N4
Tel: 1 613 748 5649
Fax: 1 613 748 5706
Telex: 053 3660

**Hong Kong**
Orienteering Association of Hong Kong
Room 1014
Sports House
1 Stadium Path
So Kon Po
Causeway Bay
Tel: 852 504 8111
Fax: 852 577 5595

**Ireland**
Irish Orienteering Association
House of Sport
Longmile Road
Walkinstown
Dublin 12
Tel: 353 1 50 98 45/1 56 90 99
Fax: 353 1 50 28 05

**Malaysia**
Malaysian Orienteering Association
55 Jalan SS 19/6H
Subang Jaya
47500 Petaling Jaya
Tel: 60 3 731 4914

**New Zealand**
New Zealand Orienteering Federation
PO Box 19312
Hamilton
Tel: 64 7 839 1214
Fax: 64 7 839 1214

**South Africa**
South African Orienteering Federation
PO Box 23 565
Claremont 7735
Tel: 27 21 658 0386
Fax: 27 21 658 0347/686 4203

**UK**
British Orienteering Federation
Riversdale
Dale Road North
Darley Dale
Matlock
Derbyshire DE4 2HX
England
Tel: 44 1629 734042
Fax: 44 1629 733769

**USA**
United States Orienteering Federation
PO Box 1444
Forest Park
GA 30051
Tel: 1 404 363 2110
Fax: 1 404 363 2110

# International control descriptions

Pictorial control descriptions are used in all international and major events.

| Symbol | Description | Symbol | Description | Symbol | Description |
|---|---|---|---|---|---|
| | marsh | | shallow | | northern |
| | small marsh | | deep | | northeastern |
| | firm ground in marsh | | overgrown | | upper |
| | well | | open | | lower |
| | source | | rocky | | middle |
| | open land | | marshy | | between |
| | semi open land | | sandy | | |
| | forest corner | | coniferous | | steep bank |
| | clearing | | deciduous | | quarry |
| | thicket | | end | | earthbank, dam |
| | felled area | | bend | | terrace |
| | vegetation boundary | | junction | | spur |
| | copse | | crossing | | rib |
| | road | | | | re-entrant |
| | path | 5.5 | height in metres | | gully |
| | narrow ride | 8×3 | length/width in metres | | dry ditch |
| | wall | | | | hill |
| | fence | | northern side | | knoll |
| | foot bridge | | northwest edge | | saddle |
| | building | | east corner (inside the angle) | | depression |
| | ruin | | southwest corner | | small depression |
| | tower | | southern tip | | pit |
| | shooting platform | | western part | | cliff |
| | fodder rack | | upper part (head) | | bare rock |
| | rock pillar | | lower part (foot) | | cave |
| | single tree | | on the top of | | boulder |
| | salt lick | | southern foot | | boulder field |
| | tree root | | at the foot | | stony ground |
| | boundary stone | | (direction not specified) | | cairn |
| | charcoal burning ground | | | | lake |
| | ant hill | | refreshments | | pond |
| | broken ground | | radio controls | | waterhole |
| | special feature | | manned control | | stream |
| | special feature | | first aid | | ditch |

A sample description sheet from a W55A course.

| Class | | | Course length | | | Climbing | |
|---|---|---|---|---|---|---|---|
| W55A | | | 4.3 km | | | 105m | |
| 1 | 98 | | ᴍ | | 2 | ʟ | |
| 2 | 72 | | V | | | | |
| 3 | 73 | ↑ | ○ | | | ·○ | ⊖ |
| 4 | 21 | | ⋀ | ⌣ | | | ⅄ |
| 5 | 27 | ‖ɬ‖ | ▲ | | 2 | ○ | |
| 6 | 28 | ⊡ | •. | | | | |
| 7 | 99 | | ⊙ | | | | |

Key to columns:

1 Control number
2 Control code
3 Which feature (if there are several)
4 The type of feature
5 Description of feature (if necessary)
6 Size of feature
7 Exact position of marker on feature
8 Extra information

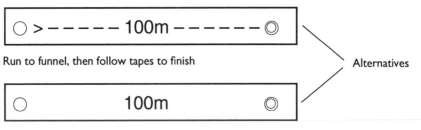

○ – – – – – – 100m – – – – – – ◎

Marked route to finish 100m

○ > – – – – – – 100m – – – – – – ◎

Run to funnel, then follow tapes to finish

○                     100m                     ◎

Navigate to finish 100m

Alternatives

# The British colour-coding system

| Colour | Length | Type of Leg | Difficulty |
|---|---|---|---|
| White | 0.5–1.5km | All routes and controls on line features | Very easy |
| Yellow | 1–2km | All routes and controls on line features | Easy |
| Orange | 2–3.5km | Easy point features. Some route choice | Medium |
| Red | 4–5km | Easy point features. Some route choice. | Medium |
| Light green | 3.5–4.5km | Contour features. Route choice | Medium hard |
| Green | 4–5km | Technically as hard as possible! Physical | Hard |
| Blue | 4.5–6km | Technically as hard as possible! Physical | Hard |
| Brown | 6km+ | Technically as hard as possible! Physical | Hard |

# IOF age classes

These are used in larger events. Orienteers enter a new age class at the start of the year in which they have that birthday. The age classes are: 10, 11, 13, 15, 17, 19, 21, 35, 40, 45, 50, 55, 60, 65, 70, 75, 80, 85, 90 (yes, there are 90-year-old orienteers who still compete!).

M or H stands for men, and W or D for women. In addition, there may be an A or B course for each age class (or sometimes Long or Short) to cater for runners of different abilities. In major events there are E, or Elite, courses for the 17, 19 and 21 classes. Thus, a D35 course would be open to women of between 35 and 39, while an H21B course would be open to men of between 21 and 34 who considered themselves insufficiently fit or experienced to tackle H21E or H21A.

# Glossary

**Attack point** Easily identified feature close to the control from which to begin a final, careful approach to the marker. On some legs it is a point of transition between fast, rough orienteering and precise, fine orienteering.

**Bearing** Direction of travel taken from the compass.

**Classes** In the larger events, competitors enter classes determined by their age, sex and ability (see page 106).

**Collecting feature** Large feature which competitors will reach should they overshoot a control.

**Continuous contact** Map-reading by following every feature on the map, when there is a need to be very precise.

**Contour-only** Orienteering with maps on which only the contours are printed. A useful training exercise.

**Contouring** Keeping to the same height across a hillside.

**Control card** Card carried by the competitor, which is punched using the needle punch at each control site as proof that the competitor has completed the course.

**Control code** Letter or number on each control marker, enabling competitor to check that they are at the correct control site before punching.

**Control descriptions** Sheet of paper carried by competitor, giving written or pictorial descriptions of each control site together with each control code.

**Control flow** Skill of approaching, punching and leaving the control marker as quickly as possible.

**Control marker** Orange-and-white, three-sided box used to mark the control site out on the course.

**Control site** Feature at the end of each leg where the control marker is sited. It is located at the centre of the control circle drawn on the map.

**Dot knoll** Hill which is too small to be mapped with a contour line, and is shown with a brown dot.

**E-punching** Electronic punching system replacing needle punches and control cards. The competitor carries a small tablet which is electronically registered at each control.

**Elite classes** Classes for the best, seeded competitors at major championships.

**Fartlek** Type of running training where the athlete can vary the pace.

**Fight** Very dense forest, sometimes referred to as 'impenetrable', and shown as dark green on the map. Best avoided!

**Fine orienteering** Precise, careful style of navigation using accurate compass and continuous map-to-ground map-reading to find difficult controls.

**Form line** Extra section of contour line drawn as a dashed brown line between two proper contours to show additional detail.

**Ground-to-map orienteering** Looking for significant features in the terrain and then finding them on the map. Useful in rough orienteering or when relocating.

**Gully** Linear cutting or depression caused by erosion or quarrying.

**Handrail** Linear feature such as a path, fence or stream which is easy to follow and helps to simplify the navigation on a leg.

**Index contour** Every fifth contour is drawn with a double-thickness line, making the overall shape of the ground easier to see on the map.

**Intervals** Training session involving periods of hard running separated by recovery periods.

**IOF** International Orienteering Federation.

**Knoll** Small hill shown with a closed contour line or a brown dot on the map.

**Leg** Section of a course between two control sites.

**Line feature** Long feature such as a path, fence or stream that can be followed easily (see Handrail).

**Loop** The part of a relay course run by each competitor in the team.

**Magnetic north** Direction in which the red end of the compass needle points. North lines on an orienteering map point to magnetic north.

**Map-to-ground** Looking at the map to form a mental picture of the ground ahead.

**Master maps** Maps at the start from which each competitor copies their course.

**Mountain marathon** Long-distance mountain orienteering, usually with teams of two running over two days and carrying lightweight camping gear.

**Negative terrain** Ground with many depressions and hollows shown with contours, and are easily confused with knolls and ridges.

**O** Short for orienteering, as in O-shoes, O-suit, O-map, O-event etc.

**OCAD** Computer program widely used for drawing orienteering maps.

**Overtraining** Physical training at a level that overloads the body and causes illness and injury.

**Pace counting** Distance estimation technique of counting how many paces have been used.

**Parallel error** Confusing one set of features for another, similar set.

**Permanent course** Course which is always set out and which can be run at any time, usually by non-competitive beginners.

**Plot** Short for photogrammetric plot: a base map specially produced from air-photos, from which an orienteering map is made.

**Pre-entry** Larger events often have to be entered in advance, or 'pre-entered'.

**Pre-marked map** Map with the course already printed on it. Standard at larger events, especially pre-entry events.

**Pre-start** Area into which the competitors are called a few minutes before they start.

**Punch** Used by the competitor to mark the control card at each control Each punch leaves a distinctive pattern of needle marks in the card as proof that the competitor has visited the right control.

**Re-entrant** Small valley or hollow in a hillside.

**Relay** Event open to teams of three or more, in which each runner completes a loop before handing on to the next runner.

**RICE** Formula for the self-treatment of sports injuries. R=Rest, I= Ice, C=Compression, E=Elevation.

**Ride** Gap in trees in a forest, such as a fire-break.

**Rough open land** Heathland or moorland terrain with few trees. Shown as pale yellow on the map.

**Rough orienteering** Collection of techniques used to cover the ground quickly on a long leg. These include using rough compass while running, and map simplification.

**Route choice** Art of choosing the best route on a particular leg.

**Runability** How easy it is to run through the terrain.

**Score events** Events where the aim is to find as many controls as possible within a time limit.

**Scribing** Way of drawing maps ready for printing, in which lines are scratched on a plastic-coated film.

**Setting the map** First principle of orienteering! Keeping the map turned so that it matches the ground at all times.

**Shadowing** Coaching technique involving following a runner through the terrain.

**Short races** Elite races with a winning time of about 25 minutes.

**Slow run** Forest where it is not quite possible to run at full speed due to the vegetation or undergrowth. Shown as light green on the map.

**Speed control** Deciding how fast to run on the basis of the difficulty of the navigation.

**Straight-line route** Direct route between controls, ignoring paths and other handrails.

**String courses** Courses for the very young, where a string or line of streamers marks the way through the terrain.

**Stub** Part of the control card that is collected at the start, as a safety check on who has started.

**Tags** Short lines drawn on to the contours on the map. They always point downhill and help the orienteer sort out up from down in areas of complex terrain.

**Terrain** Forested, heathland, moorland or farmland country which is used for orienteering.

**Terrain running** Running on rough ground, as opposed to paths or roads. An important aspect of orienteering fitness.

**Thumbing the map** Important and basic technique of keeping your thumb next to your position on the map.

**Trail orienteering** Orienteering for the disabled.

**Visibility** How far it is possible to see through the terrain. This will affect the difficulty of the orienteering.

**Visualization** Forming a mental picture of the ground ahead from the map.

**Walk** Dense forest where it is only possible to walk; in between 'slow run' and 'fight'. Shown as a mid-green colour on the map.

# Index

Page numbers in *italic* indicate illustrations